Part-Time Lady

also by Ann Hill Workman
COOK, CAT AND COLANDER

Ann Hill Workman

PART-TIME Lady

Illustrated by Jill Cox

ANDRE DEUTSCH

First published 1986 by André Deutsch Limited
105 Great Russell Street London WC1

Copyright © 1986 by Ann Hill Workman

British Library Cataloguing in Publication Data

Workman, Ann Hill
  Part-time lady:
  1. Office practice
  I. Title
  651'.092'4   HF5547.5

  ISBN 0–233–97860–7

Phototypeset by Multiplex techniques ltd, Orpington, Kent
Printed in Great Britain by
Ebenezer Baylis & Son Limited
Worcester

To my daughter Dinah,
for all the love and all the laughs.
'Here's bunny in your booze...'

Contents

Prologue

Larne Harbour on a bleak, windy, rainswept October morning was not an inspiring sight. Neither was I. An emotional departure from London, followed by a sleepless overnight coach journey to Scotland and a rough ferry crossing to Northern Ireland, had done their worst, emotionally and physically; a pallid, heavy-eyed hag, I scanned the quayside fruitlessly for a welcoming face. The few hardy souls in view, huddled together like wet sheep, revealed no familiar figure. Where was the lean, bronzed Irishman from whom I had so reluctantly parted last summer? Probably saw me coming, I thought gloomily, and very sensibly hightailed it for the hills, appalled at what he'd let himself in for in a moment of mad, sun-drenched August euphoria. Oh well, no sense in staying on the ferry for the return journey; my boats were well and truly burnt behind me and in any case I hadn't got enough money. My ticket was, after all, paid right through to Belfast; might as well disembark and sample the delights of Ulster now that I was here.

I hoisted my suitcase, shoulder-bag and tatty assortment of bursting plastic bags, clutched my trusty skunk coat more tightly around me – it was too bulky to pack and doubled as a duvet in an emergency – and tottered down the gangplank, peering again, hopefully, at those waiting below. I was too vain, even in that pitiful condition, to put my glasses on, and anyway I'd have needed windscreen wipers. As I set foot on wet land, a figure swathed in oilskins detached itself from the bedraggled flock and moved towards me. Barely visible between a high roll-neck sweater and what appeared to be a purple knitted tea cosy pulled well down over the ears was the tip of a nose. It matched the tea cosy exactly. Two eyes, slitted to keep out the sleet, were just discernible, neatly arranged one each side of the nose. At least the creature was of vaguely human aspect.

As it shuffled nearer, it even seemed a little familiar. Something about the nose? The eyes? There wasn't much else to go on, but little flickers of recognition stirred turgidly somewhere deep in my mental recesses, stupefied by lack of sleep and nervous tension exacerbated by a steady overnight diet of black coffee, cigarettes and Valium. Could this be the man for whom I had left England, home and beauty, not to mention family, a well-paid job and the joys of Selfridge's every Saturday? The apparition spoke, with difficulty, through the folds of its sweater.

'I was so afraid you'd change your mind at the last minute,' it said, and enveloped me in a great, rib-crushing hug. It was Himself! An enormous wave of relief swept over me, and we clung together in a soggy, ecstatic embrace. I may have been a stranger in a strange land, but it felt like coming home.

This highly romantic and enjoyable state of affairs lasted precisely as long as it took us to travel, hand clasped tightly in frozen hand, by bus to Belfast. In between gazing besottedly into my beloved's slightly bloodshot eyes – he had spent the previous evening prudently soaking up Dutch courage to face the ordeal of either (a) my non-arrival or (b) my arrival – I gazed out of the window and

tried to appreciate how green the countryside would be if only I could see it through the downpour. I was very hungry, very cold and very tired; reaction was setting in, and the outskirts of Belfast didn't do a lot to raise my spirits. It wasn't exactly the prettiest side of town. Never mind, I told myself, not long to go now. We'll soon be at Himself's flat and everything will be lovely. And, as I drew comfort from this happy prospect and tried to ignore the agony caused by wearing fashion boots for a straight fourteen hours – they were too tight to remove unaided – we arrived at the coach terminal.

There's No Place Like Home

The first shock was not being able to find a taxi. The second was having to trudge to the flat, lugging my baggage between us. By now I felt true sisterhood with the Little Mermaid who, for love of a landsman, forsook her native habitat; not only did my feet feel as if I were walking on knives with every step, but I was soaked to the skin, skunk and all. The third shock was The Flat.

I knew Himself *had* a flat – he'd mentioned it in passing from time to time in the hundreds of letters we'd exchanged during the previous fifteen months. Two-bedroomed, he'd said, a big kitchen, but of course he hadn't really gone into any detail; men don't, do they, and anyway we had far more important things to write about. I'd sort of taken it for granted that it was a counterpart of my own two-bedroomed flat in London – central heating, double glazing, fitted kitchen, fitted carpets, built-in wardrobes, answer phone so that you could check on callers before you let them into the building and a spy-hole in your front door so that you could check on them again, just to make sure they were who they said they were. Nothing fancy, just a nice modern flat in a nice modern purpose-built block surrounded by a strip of grass and the odd tree or two. So it was just as well I was already stunned by exhaustion when he finally stopped trudging, put my case down in a puddle, disentangled a key from his pocket and exclaimed thankfully, 'Here we are!'

The house leaned outwards over the street at an alarming angle. Then, as well as inclining forwards, bits of it seemed to have lurched sideways independently. If a lintel felt like sloping to the right, a doorsill to the left, they just did. In a phrase, the whole building showed a disturbing lack of *esprit de corps*. Only the shops on either side of it appeared to prevent the whole thing from subsiding on to the pavement in a welter of separate bricks. It was my first sight of that Belfast phenomenon, the equivalent of the house built on shifting sands – the house built on boggy foundations.

Himself unlocked the lopsided front door, pushed it open with an effort and ushered me into the entrance hall. Gingerly, I picked my way past four bicycles, several heaps of sports gear, a bucket and two planks and made it to

the stairs. 'Where's your *flat*?' I whimpered, as I stepped on the fourth stair and heard for the first time the ear-splitting creak which was to become so familiar over the next year. 'At the top,' he said cheerfully.

We trailed up the first flight, catching our toes on dislodged stair rods, turned the corner and were suddenly in the midst of what appeared to be someone's home; a kitchen door stood open, pop music issued from a sitting room, a girl in a pink shortie nightie dashed across the landing into a bathroom. Himself gave her the time of day politely – I was too shattered for speech – and we began the assault on the second flight. Where's his front *door*, I thought desperately. All I could think about was closing it behind me, collapsing, and getting those bloody boots off. We rounded another corner, climbed a final and thankfully short stair and we were there. He didn't *have* a front door. He had an Attic.

A big attic, I grant you. Two bedrooms, I also grant you. Five rooms in all, actually, because there was a sitting room, a bathroom and a kitchen as well. They were large – in fact, as any house agent worth his salt would doubtless have told you, the place had great potential. All of it unrealised. Only one bedroom was habitable; the kitchen, bathroom and uninhabitable bedroom were windowless save for a skylight, and the other rooms had tiny dormer windows so high up that the only view was of sky and the underside of the occasional pigeon. It was cold, it was dusty, it was basic, there was a mouse hole in the kitchen wainscoting. It was, of course, the typical base camp of a lifelong bachelor dedicated to the outdoor life. But I'd never met one before, and it was all too much, on top of everything else. I took one horrified look round and fell on to the nearest bed. 'Oh, it's *awful*,' I wailed and burst into floods of tears.

Faced with this childish and ungrateful reaction to the opportunity to share his precious home, Himself could have been forgiven for turfing me out again, bag and baggage, on to the rainy streets. Instead, he repressed an understandable urge to spank my bottom – a pity, really – and did the essential things to comfort me in the circumstances. He hauled my boots off, put the kettle on and cuddled me, in that order, and after that, things could only get better.

I had arrived on a Saturday morning, so of course the first thing to be done, after I had finished my cathartic outburst, was to introduce me to that holy of holies, the epicentre of Himself's world, the Rugby Club. Would I like to go and watch that afternoon's game? Frankly, I'd much rather have stayed in bed and devised a game of our own, but he was so keen for me to go and I felt I should make up for my previous pettiness, so the Rugby Club it was. I'd had a warming bath by this time and put a new face on and was looking a bit more presentable than the whey-faced, half-drowned rat of the morning. But it was still bitterly cold outside, although the rain had stopped, so I had to drag on the boots again, plus my stretch jeans and a heavy sweater, and we trotted off, with me trying hard to remember whether or not I'd ever seen a rugby game before.

By the time we got to the club, the game was in progress on the far side of the grounds; Himself hurried me over the grass in his eagerness not to miss a single moment of the thrilling play, and in seconds my precious, if painful, boots were plastered with mud to the instep. The four-inch heels didn't help, in that kind of terrain, and before we reached the ramshackle spectators' stand I had ricked my ankle twice and had to be lifted bodily out of the soggy earth three times when my heels sank in and impaled me to the spot. The stretch jeans, too, were a mistake; they were obviously only meant to be stood up in, possibly leaning studiedly against something. Walked about in, the seams did terrible things to unmentionable parts of my anatomy; I began to fear for my future ability to ride a bike, amongst other things. I might never dance again, either.

What I know about rugby, even now, would barely cover the head of a pin; what I knew then would have fitted nicely on to a very small microdot. I stood shivering in the lee of the stand and watched these great hairy idiots thundering up and down in a sea of mud, occasionally flinging themselves to the ground and rising even less recognisable as human beings. Now and then they would all cluster together, heads down, for what appeared to be either a friendly natter or a trial of strength. I assumed it to be the former; from the way they were gripping each other in the most intimate places, they must have been very good friends indeed.

In the stand behind us was an assortment of spectators, all men. I was the only female present, and it didn't take me long to work out why. All the other wives and girlfriends had more sense than to spend their Saturday afternoons like this. Doubtless they were all at home, toasting their toes in front of the fire, wading into the tea and biccies and getting their sport the pleasant way, on the television. I tried to be interested in what was going on, but it wasn't easy. From time to time all the men, including Himself, would suddenly roar together, like a pride of lions, and proffer incomprehensible advice to those on the field. 'Play the *ball*' – I thought they were, they had nothing else to play with except each other – '*Heave*' – not surprising, considering the amount of mud they must be ingesting – 'A great wee hooker, that!' – I looked round in vain for a small lady of the night. Oh, I *was* glad when it was all over and we could stagger back over the morass and into the warmth of the bar . . . I was given a glass of Guinness – a taste I rapidly acquired – and left to get on with it while the game was analysed move by move by all the alickadoos (ex-players now over the hill) who would, naturally, have done it all differently and far, far better. It was nice to go home, and turn on the telly for a bit of culture, even if it was only the Dukes of Hazzard.

The real ordeal of the day, however, still lay ahead of me. Everyone had left the club bar only in order to get ready to return later in the evening, when the company would be augmented by the strictly social members. And by Himself's circle of friends, all of whom I would be meeting for the first time. I did my makeup yet again, literally putting on a brave face, trying to strike a suitable balance between too much paint, which would confirm their suspicions that I was a scarlet woman, and too little, which would make me look like death warmed up. 'Have you told them what I'm like?' I queried anxiously, rummaging through my suitcase for something as flattering, yet modest, as possible. 'Oh, I mentioned you were coming,' Himself said, 'I *think*,' he added doubtfully. 'Yes, but did you tell them what I was *like*?' I persisted, rejecting the crimson catsuit and settling for the high-necked cream wool. I didn't want to get there and find they were expecting someone totally different. 'I said you were tall,' he replied. And that was all. It wasn't much help.

Going back into the bar was one of the hardest things I've ever done. Ulster society is very close-knit; everyone has known everyone else since the year dot, and I was a complete stranger. I was terribly grateful for my shortsightedness – all I'd be able to see would be a comforting blurry mass until I got up close, so I wouldn't know whether or not anyone was staring at me. Himself steered me through the merry throng until we got to the hallowed corner where his friends were assembled. It was worse than going for a job interview; more like being summoned to the headmaster's study when you don't know what you've done.

I needn't have worried. I was introduced all round, as usual instantly forgetting every name, a stool was produced for me to sit on – just as well, because my knees were like water – and a glass of reviving fluid was thrust into my hand. 'Would you look at that now, your hands are shaking!' exclaimed a lovely large cuddly man, steadying the glass for me and probably deciding I had DTs. 'I'm terrified, that's why,' I explained. 'I'm absolutely petrified . . .' His response was a big warm hug round my shoulders, and from then on we all got on like a house on fire. I certainly didn't feel like a stranger by the time we got home that night; I felt like a slightly inebriated woman who'd just made a whole lot of terrific new friends. The 'crack' had ranged from literature to history, with side excursions into personalities, politics and dozens of other subjects, and a heated discussion on transubstantiation for good measure. Rugby hadn't even been mentioned.

I had, however, been more than a little intrigued by one or two *sotto voce* comments that had floated to my ears during the evening. Like 'Well, wonders never cease! He must have something going for him that we don't know about . . .' And 'D'you mean she's really come over to *live* with him?' And, most intriguing of all, 'I'm glad to see he's got a halfway decent one this time, anyway.' What did they mean, *this time*?

* * *

On the following Monday, of course, Himself had to return to work and I was left alone in the attic, feeling like Mariana in the Moated Grange. Isolated at the top of the empty house, I had a thoroughly enjoyable time ransacking the desk and learning more about my beloved in an hour than I'd learnt in the whole previous year. Having exhausted the possibilities of that, I moved on to the bookcase and was fascinated to find that most of the hundreds of books were anchored securely to the wall by spiders' webs, in the manner of ancient volumes chained to their stands in university libraries. I had already discovered, as I have recounted elsewhere,* that Himself kept seventeen shoes under his bed, each one cosily ensconced in its own little protective jacket of grey fluff, and now I noticed that the carpet, too, was grey. In fact, almost everything seemed to be grey. I licked my finger and rubbed the carpet experimentally. Instantly, a great wodge of hairy dust adhered to my finger, revealing a glimpse of green pile. I decided that the moment for action had come. One of my rare moods of domesticity swept over me; I would clean the place thoroughly, from end to end and top to bottom, and surprise Himself with my housewifely virtue when he got home.

Three hours later I was still at it, and could now identify completely with Hercules labouring in the Augean Stables. Himself possessed no vacuum cleaner, no dusters, no bucket, no broom. Just a dustpan and balding brush, an ossified packet of Flash under the sink, and a washing-up bowl. On my hands and knees, determined not to be beaten by a mere carpet, I raised great heaps of fluff that resembled the giant tumbleweeds so familiar from

---

* See Ann Hill Workman's first book *Cook, Cat and Colander* (Deutsch, 1984).

Westerns; wielding what I took to be a discarded pair of underpants (I found out later they were his second-best ones) I dusted and wiped and scoured; using a succession of eight bowls of hot detergent I washed down the banisters; bravely, I excavated under the beds but never found the eighteenth shoe. At last, totally knackered, I dried my sodden hands, put my aching legs up on the sofa and rewarded myself with a large whisky. Himself's footsteps echoed on the stairs, and I preened myself with what energy I had left and waited for the gasps of appreciation.

He strode into the sitting room and stopped dead. 'Where on earth did you get this green carpet from?' he said.

While there were definite drawbacks to the attic flat, there were advantages, too. For one thing, you couldn't possibly be overlooked except by descending parachutists, or helicopter pilots with binoculars. For another, the occupants of the rooms on the floor below us turned out to be a delightful bunch; a mixed bag of boys and girls, all students, whose radio and record player we could benefit from without going to the expense of buying one for ourselves, and whose frilly briefs hanging in the yard brightened Himself's day. They were chatty and friendly, and their social life was hectic; I'd get back from shopping to find a pencilled note pinned to the front door informing anyone who was interested that they were all away to the Bot or the Egg – two popular local hostelries – and would welcome the company of anyone who cared to join them, and on other evenings sounds of revelry would float tantalisingly up the stairs. I got pretty friendly with the pink-nightie girl, who delighted me by confiding over an afternoon coffee that they had all been so surprised when I had arrived – 'We always thought of him as that nice quiet elderly man upstairs,' she explained, with the candour of youth which regards anyone over forty as approaching the brink of senility. Himself wasn't quite so delighted when I told him, though; but it didn't stop him from appreciating their washing-line. It's when they *stop* looking that you should start worrying.

A further advantage was the amount of space we had. The second bedroom, unusable because of damp and the fact that all the wallpaper had fallen off, came in extremely handy for all sorts of bits and pieces and obviously had for years past. Himself had stuff stored there which kept me occupied for many a happy afternoon, reading his school reports and sorting through ancient bank statements which showed that he was £1 14s 2d overdrawn. After my possessions arrived from London by carrier, you couldn't get into the place. Packing cases, tea chests, cardboard boxes and portable wardrobes were crammed in to join all the rest of the stuff and you needed crampons and a grapnel to get from one side of the room to the other. I was thankful I'd only brought the bare essentials – my books, my clothes, my collection of 134 cats made from every substance known to man, boxes full of old letters, birthday cards, telegrams of congratulation on the births of my children, photographs ... all the paraphernalia without which I couldn't live. They were the record of my life.

There were one or two other essentials which were lacking from Himself's cosy little eyrie. Like a fridge, for example; he'd never felt the need for one, because in the summer he was rarely in the place and in the winter everything froze solid anyway. After a couple of weeks of turned milk and sour sausages I'd had enough and within days a small fridge had been installed in the wasteland of the kitchen. The television had to be changed, too; my eyes went funny from watching a flickery black and white picture on those evenings when Himself was out and there was no other entertainment to hand, and I was shortly able to enjoy watching Elsie Tanner in glorious colour. I didn't go so far as to get a vacuum cleaner, though; I reckoned one sweeping every few years was as much as the carpet, and I, could stand. Besides, I didn't want to expose Himself to too much of a culture shock; as it was, the poor man was having to accustom himself to sharing his bed, board and bathroom with a woman for the first time in his life. On a long-term, all-day-every-day basis, that is. As far as *I* knew, anyway.

This sudden acquisition of a flatmate was something that had worried me considerably. Would it be awkward, would it prove difficult? Would we get on each other's nerves and in each other's hair? I'd anticipated a lengthy period of mutual adjustment, the usual establishing of compromises, the gradual realisations that one's best-beloved is a grouch in the mornings or hogs the bathroom or leaves the sink in a revolting state. I might discover that Himself, in his own environment, had distressing habits of which I had been unaware. Worse still, he could well discover *my* distressing habits. It'll take a while, I warned myself, for us to shake down together. We had known each other for a total of fifteen months; but out of that time, we'd only actually been in each other's company for a grand total of eight days – and that not in one stretch or even two, but in dribs and drabs of a couple of days here, an hour or so there.

But it was a revelation; he didn't seem to have any annoying habits, and he either didn't notice or didn't mind mine. We meshed in together like well-oiled cogwheels. We didn't even get in each other's way in the bathroom.

It was like living with yourself, only much more fun. Even the fact that I am a lark and he is an owl worked to our advantage. I rise in the mornings disgustingly bright-eyed and bushy-tailed; I even sing, which might have driven a lesser man to homicide. Himself was just filled with wonder that anyone could speak, let alone sing, at the crack of dawn. For the first few weeks he even took turns, nobly, to brew the early morning tea without which he is unable to articulate either his limbs or his vocal chords, but after a while I took pity on him as he stumbled blindly about in the kitchen, filling the kettle by feel and pouring boiling water all over his feet, and his turn of duty was shifted to the weekends when we could rise at a civilised hour, like midday. For my part, I was astonished at his ability not only to sit up and watch the late-night movie, but to be chattily conversational for hours after it was over; an impossible achievement for me, accustomed as I was to feeling pangs of guilt over wild living and lost sleep if I got to bed later than ten-thirty. In self defence, I took to retiring for a quick lie-down and a bit of a snooze directly after dinner, until about nine-thirty when, in Belfast, it is time for people to start to think about perhaps preparing themselves to get ready to go out . . . Not that it always worked out as intended; sometimes the quick lie-down developed into a bit of something more interesting than a snooze and I would spend the rest of the evening propping my eyelids open with matches and concentrating furiously to prevent the surrounding voices fading inexorably away into the distance.

Another of the worry-making things that had exercised my mind before joining Himself was that, during our extensive correspondence, he had once let slip the intelligence that he never kept alcohol in the house. My heart sank. Having lived a large part of my adult life in Africa,

I was firmly and happily in the habit of imbibing at least a couple of sundowners before dinner every night. Had been ever since I was seventeen, always (given the luck and the money) would be. Should I, *could* I, commit myself to a man who thus eschewed alcohol and its concomitant pleasures in the home? Could I become a small-sherry lady, a port-at-Christmas person, a placer of the hand over the glass when the wine bottles circulated? It's amazing how your judgement can be warped by love; I decided that, even with this sad flaw in his character, he was worth the sacrifice. I've never liked lunchtime drinking; I would just have to learn not to like dinnertime drinking, either. I could always keep a bottle of Wincarnis under the sink – purely for medicinal emergencies, of course, like getting home from work faint with exhaustion.

Once again, I was worrying needlessly. It took me exactly five days in residence to realise that he kept no drink in the house because he was never there. He was out every night. Down at the club. Drinking. Monday night was Monday Club, a come-hell-or-high-water commitment to a small circle of stalwarts who had sustained the club profits through dungeon, fire and sword at the height of the Troubles. Tuesday was his popping-over-to-the-Regency night. Wednesday was Up to the Tennis Club Night. Thursday was Down to the Yacht Club Night. Friday was the Rugby Club, in a sort of limbering-up exercise for Saturday, which was also a Rugby Night only fiercer. Sunday, he was back at the tennis club again. So, as he pointed out, there was little point in his keeping alcohol in the flat. 'If I did,' he reasoned, 'I'd only drink it.'

Now that he was lumbered with a dependant, however, and moreover one who was as averse as he to missing out on a round, a few changes again had to be made. Going out to drink, delightful though it was, now cost him twice as much, and while *he* was perfectly happy with this arrangement, it wouldn't be long before his bank manager wasn't. Either we had to cut down on the going out, or we had to augment our income. Preferably both. Monday Club being inviolate, and Saturday practically compulsory, we settled for Wednesday as our other night out and scrubbed the rest except for special occasions. Besides, he didn't have to go out for company now he had lovely old me, and it was much cosier sitting at home by the fire with a friendly bottle of something and not having to brave the wet and windy streets of Belfast. Or so I told him, and he pretended he believed me.

Augmenting the income was of prime importance. The cost of living is frighteningly high in Ulster, more expensive in many respects than London; I had to get a job of some sort, and quickly. A week of domesticity and long quiet days in the silent house was quite enough for me; I began to hear funny noises on the stairs and to imagine I heard the distant front door opening stealthily. Rushing up and down the staircase to check might have done a power of good to my thighs, but it was murder on my nerves; I expected to be confronted by a masked gunman at the very least every time, but usually it was just the postman desperately trying to shove something through the dilapidated letter box. The charms of housework palled with their usual rapidity, and anyway I had to take the plunge some time; so, armed with a list of all the temping agencies and a careful selection of suitable references – some going back so far that they resembled papyrus – I began the search for work.

Hurrah for the High Life

It would be my first experience of temping – if, that is, I could successfully con an agency into employing me. Goodness knows I'd had enough different jobs. Apart from my recent years as a live-in cook housekeeper (chronicled in *Cook, Cat and Colander*) I'd done secretarial work for, amongst others, chartered accountants, shipping agencies, colonial government departments, a large charity, a language school, a big hotel, a university department of experimental psychology and the probation service – the last two having a lot more in common than might meet the eye at first glance. Also, there is no truth in the commonly held belief that accountants are a dour and bloodless lot, devoted to the decimal and only roused to passion by profit and loss accounts. 'A trial balance' can take on a quite new and unsuspected meaning when attempted at the annual Christmas party. And the probation service can open your eyes to things you never imagined in your wildest dreams. All these jobs had, however, been on a permanent basis – at least, I'd always started off with that intention, even if it hadn't always ended up that way. And they'd all had their moments. Take the hotel job, for instance.

'Under-secretary to manager of large Cotswold hotel,' the

19

advertisement had said. Glamorous, I thought, visualising a gay cosmopolitan clientèle of rich American and European tourists, flinging their money about tip-wise with mad abandon and no idea of the value of English currency. 'Part-time,' it said. Ideal; I had two school-age children and needed to be home before they were. And best of all, it said 'Meals provided'. Terrific, I decided; with any luck, my housekeeping bills would be cut at the proverbial stroke. I applied for it immediately, typing the letter neatly on the machine at my current job, slipping it unobtrusively in amongst the office mail and thus maintaining my habitual practice of not leaving an unsatisfactory job until a new one is safely secured, on the premise that any job is better than none.

An interview was granted. I took the afternoon off work to go to the dentist, and presented myself at the appointed time clean, bright and only slightly puffed as a result of having had to cycle five miles into the country and then ask directions which had sent me two miles back again. The head porter, leering ominously, escorted me to the manager's office. As soon as I was ushered in, my spirits rose by leaps and bounds; it was beautifully large and luxurious. So was the manager; my spirits rose even higher. He was French, he was charming, he was handsome. We had a simply lovely interview, and at the end of it the job was mine. I was to start the next month, nine to two-thirty, five days a week, at a wage of five shillings an hour. Plus breakfast and lunch. I cycled home trailing clouds of glory, my head full of delicious visions of the manager and myself closeted intimately among the deep-pile carpet and velvet upholstery, planning gourmet banquets for the jet-set, perhaps sharing a perfectly chilled bottle of The Widow for elevenses before I trotted off to toy with a slice or two of smoked salmon, followed, if pressed, by a small

Tournedos Rossini. You must understand that I was very young then, and very romantic.

The lovely visions sustained me through the never particularly happy period of working out my notice, clearing my desk of spare stockings, old paperbacks and broken eye-pencils, bequeathing my pot plants to favoured colleagues, lashing out on a bottle of British sherry for a farewell drink, and leaving those with whom I'd worked for the past couple of years. It's always awful, leaving a job; for a certain length of time, months or years, you've spent more time with your workmates than you have at home with your family. You hear all their most intimate secrets, their worries, their joys; you know their families and their friends, albeit at second hand. You get accustomed to coping with Shirley's premenstrual tension, you comfort the office junior through a succession of adolescent heartbreaks, you commiserate with Fran over her awful mother and worse mother-in-law. You even tolerate Val's constant sniffing. And all of a sudden, unless you live close by or are the kind of person who attends school reunions, you rarely see them again. A whole new lot of people have to be got used to – and have to get used to you, too.

And there was a lot of getting-used-to waiting for me at the hotel. Reality, as distinct from my rosy imaginings, set in even before I got there. Anxious to look the part of the sophisticated secretary and, just incidentally, to impress the Gorgeous Gaul, I dressed in what was then the accepted ideal – the ubiquitous little black costume, with pristine white blouse, discreet string of (Woolworth's) pearls with matching clip-on earrings, dark seamed stockings and black court shoes. The skirt half of the costume was tight, the jacket was nipped in at the waist, the shoes had three-inch heels. My hair was rigidly lacquered into an immaculate beehive, like a pile of varnished Brillo pads. I looked terrific. I looked out of the window. It was coming down like stair rods. And I had three miles to go on my bike. Resignedly, I reached for my plastic cycling cape.

By the time I reached work, my suspender belt had worn a welt into my hips, my blouse was sticking clammily to my back under the jacket and cape, I'd laddered a stocking on the pedal and the beehive had lurched drunkenly to one side. I did the best I could to remedy matters in the staff toilet but it was a bit disheartening; there's not much you can do about a laddered stocking unless you carry a spare, and beehives couldn't be taken down and re-erected. Between visits to the hairdresser, you slept sitting up, or wrapped your head in crêpe lavatory paper every night. So I could only make emergency repairs, shoving in a few more hairpins and going berserk with the lacquer, and holding the whole listing edifice upright until it set like ferrous concrete, before presenting myself for duty.

I made my way through the vacuum-loud early morning corridors and, pausing outside the manager's office, I ran a final reassuring hand over my coiffure to make sure it was relatively intact and arranged my face into what I hoped was an expression combining efficiency, dedication and irresistible allure. I knocked briskly yet gently upon the panelling and, without waiting for a reply, entered in best charm-school manner, reaching round behind me to close the door quietly, thus avoiding turning my back and enabling me to stun the Gorgeous Gaul with a full-frontal aspect while concealing the stocking ladder, which was at the back of my calf.

Had my forehead not been rigid with spray, my eyebrows would have shot up to my hairline. Where was my latter-day Charles Boyer? The figure before me bore more resemblance to Charles Laughton, in one of his less benign roles. Six foot tall, three wide and two deep, seventeen stone at a conservative guess and all of it encased in mauve polyester. I was confronting Venetia, the manager's Head Secretary, and she was an awesome sight.

'Good morning,' she ground out, in a voice like bottles being crushed under a steamroller. 'You're late. We begin work here at nine, not two minutes past.' It wasn't an auspicious start to my career in the ritzy catering trade. Not only was she physically overwhelming, she was a slave-driver where work was concerned, and what Venetia wanted, she got. What she wanted from me was full-time work in part-time hours for part-time pay – and believe me, she made sure it was forthcoming. She also made it quite plain that I was the *under*-secretary, and what I was going to be under was not the boss, but her. Half an hour into my first day's work I felt as if I were going down for the third time. Gone irrevocably were my lovely dreams of cosy collaborations over menus and receptions; gone my innocent aspirations towards mingling with the rich and famous. That was *her* prerogative.

Without any further light conversation, she spent the first hour of our acquaintance dictating, at machine-gun speed and with a heavy South African accent, a series of routine letters which I frantically attempted to memorise. I knew I'd never be able to read back my shorthand, which is idiosyncratic at the best of times and tends, under stress, to resemble something produced by a decapitated hen with inky feet executing its death throes all over the page. At ten o'clock, by which time I had writer's cramp, hysterical blindness and amnesia, she called a halt and announced that I could go for my breakfast. It was at this point that I discovered that gone, too, were my hopes of any freeloading of delicious gourmet meals. *My* position only entitled me to eat in the staff kitchen, it transpired. And *that* was something altogether different from the hotel dining room.

Venetia directed me dismissively towards a door leading off the corridor. It led me into a rabbit warren of passages, none of them particularly clean and all of them redolent of onions, boiled cabbage and that unique aroma of over-used cooking fat which was once graphically described to me as fried armpit. A lad in a grubby apron came to my rescue eventually, after I had twice found myself out in the back yard with the dustbins. He led me through a swing door and there it was: the staff kitchen – in all its awful glory.

The place was packed. Chambermaids and waitresses, with their shoes off, eased their varicose veins by putting their feet up; kitchen porters, their overalls decorated with nameless stains, slurped pint mugs of dark brown tea; waiters, grateful that the breakfast rush in the restaurant was over, sat in their shirt sleeves and dealt with their own breakfasts; pimply bellboys demolished vast piles of fried bread and sausages. There was a shrieking roar of conversation, a deafening clatter of plates and pans and cutlery. Over all hung a pall of cigarette smoke, cooking fumes and steam. It was Bedlam set in Dante's Inferno.

Faced with this, I nearly backed out of the door again – it was terrifying and I couldn't see properly because of not wearing my glasses. But the lure of a free meal, even here, was too strong. I tried to be unobtrusive, sliding along the greasy walls in search of an empty chair, but I stuck out like a sore thumb, what with the little black suit and the pearls and all. Under the unabashed and critical gaze of what felt like a hundred pairs of eyes, I panicked; and instead of taking my time, reached blindly for the

first vacant seat. It was at a table occupied by three middle-
aged kitchen porters, who all immediately transferred the
intense interest they had been concentrating on their food
to me.

'Wossis then?' the middle one of the three enquired of
the mate seated on his right hand. ' 'Oos this young lady
then? 'As she lost 'er way, Bert?' His mate stared at me

speculatively, picking bits of bacon out of a molar with a blackened fingernail. 'Slummin', I shouldn't wonder,' he surmised. The last of the trio put down the knife with which he had been ingesting his baked beans, burped gently and added his fourpenn'orth. 'Bit of all right, though,' he commented. 'Bit of a turn up for the books, eh?'

In the face of this shameless sexual harassment I should, of course, have frozen them with an icy glance before putting them firmly in their place with a few well chosen words. Venetia would have, with no trouble at all. What I did do was to drop my handbag on the floor, blush scarlet and, in a voice rendered unnaturally high and genteel by sheer nerves, proffer the information that I was the new under-secretary. 'Ho, har we then,' responded the baked-bean eater, adopting an excruciatingly refined accent. 'There we was, thinkin' you was one of the *guests*, not one of the 'umble *workers*. Ho dearie me, Cedric,' he continued, addressing Bert, 'Hi can see as 'ow we'll 'ave to mind our manners. Kindly refrain from pickin' your teeth with your fingers, Cedric. From now hon, do what the toffs do. Use a fork.'

Overcome by his own wit, he guffawed merrily, disclosing a great many yellow teeth and the fact that he hadn't swallowed all the beans. I gathered my courage. 'Where can I get some breakfast?' I whispered, surveying the detritus of their plates to see what was on offer. It was no good letting them bully me; I was starving, and I only had half an hour to do something about it. The man in the middle leapt theatrically to his feet. 'Hi will fetch the chef personally, madam, hif you will kindly 'ang on a mo,' he cried, and pushing between the tables with a '*Hex*cuse me, *hif* you don't mind, madam wishes to place a horder,' he vanished into the wreaths of steam to emerge moments later dragging the cook behind him. 'There you are, madam,' he panted triumphantly, 'your hevery wish is my command!'

'Wotcher want?' said the cook, a wispy little man in sinisterly stained apron and a tall hat that had wilted all to one side, like a collapsing soufflé. 'Wotcher got?' I replied, falling into the vernacular. It was catching. 'Bacon egg sausage baked beans fried bread tomato,' he reeled off in a monotone. 'An' chips, of course.' 'Yes please,' I said, and had the satisfaction of seeing the Terrible Trio stunned into a silence which was broken only when my meal arrived. They all leaned forward to watch me as I tackled the mountainous plateful. 'You won't 'urt if you get outside that lot, gel,' said Bert, with a new note of respect in his voice. I did get outside it, finishing up with two slices of toast and marmalade and a mug of dark tea, too. 'Nothin' much wrong with your appetite, anyway,' said the baked-bean eater. ' 'Ere, 'ave a fag, love.' I was in; accepted. But Bert was wrong about not hurting. By the time I lurched back to the corridors of power, my waistband was killing me.

Not that I was allowed to stalk the corridors of power very often. Far from it; I did my work in a little back office, with a dead geranium and a glorious view of a brick wall two feet from my window. Apart from the odd occasions on which I took dictation in the manager's office – usually from Venetia – I spent my whole day there, only emerging to join my three knights in mucky overalls for meals. I would roll back from yet another glorious greasy blow-out to find Venetia, fresh from the dining room, sitting waiting impatiently for me, tapping her fingers on the desk and putting the flimsy chair in severe peril. She didn't approve of my friends in the staff kitchen.

She thought I was lowering myself and that I should have insisted on eating in solitary splendour, aloof from the rabble. I was glad that her sense of propriety didn't extend as far as inviting me to join her at meals; it was far more fun downstairs and I wouldn't have got nearly as much to eat. She asked me on that first morning what I'd had for breakfast and when I told her she shuddered all over like a massive mauve blancmange, closed her eyes to indicate her revulsion and told me that I should have had what she always had – grapefruit, melba toast and black coffee. 'If you cerry on eating like *thet*,' she said with Johannesburgian distaste, 'you'll get *fet*.' That's rich, coming from you, I thought. Over the next few months I derived a good deal of perverse pleasure from recounting my intake to her in detail. And I never put on an ounce; it must have been all the cycling. My housekeeping budget got slightly fatter though. After two sessions a day with the Terrible Trio, I couldn't face a thing at night.

The little office was terribly claustrophobic, so I was quite agreeable when, a few weeks into my time there, Venetia transferred me from the office to do a stint on the hotel switchboard. One of the girls had left suddenly, for no apparent reason, and the remaining telephonist couldn't cope alone. I'd never worked on a switchboard before; it would be a new experience and at least there'd be something different to look at as a change from the brick wall. Also, there was a view from the telephone room into the reception area. At last I'd be in a position to see the rich, the famous and the beautiful; I might even get to speak to them, if only on the phone.

I really enjoyed my sessions on the switchboard, even if the guests didn't. It was one of the old-fashioned sort, with rows and rows of blinking dolls' eyes that flickered up and down alarmingly and made a constant mind-numbing clatter. No wonder the other girl had left so precipitately. It was very disconcerting being winked at all day, and some of the eyes positively leered, lowering their little metal lids with a slow suggestiveness that was unnervingly humanoid. Being inexperienced, I had a field day at the expense of the poor guests, plugging the wrong people in to each other, disconnecting business calls at moments of prime importance, cutting off long-distance conversations in full flow and generally making myself useful. Heaven knows how many deals went unconcluded, how many orders were lost, how many love affairs were nipped in the bud due to my ministrations. My best ever effort happened when the Australian cricketers were in residence. The entire team, suddenly assailed by homesickness, decided to ring their families who all lived in remote places with names like Woolloomoolloo and Bangalonga. It took me absolute ages and a great deal of patience to get them all through to the right person; lonely postmistresses in the outback cranked handles and alerted party lines to interesting incoming calls – even so far away, I could hear all the neighbouring receivers being picked up – and wives and mothers had to be called in from laundering sheep or gelding kangaroos or whatever. Over the wires I could hear the vast distances humming and echoing; it sounded like the music of the spheres.

At last, each caller was in touch with his personal callee, no doubt arranging for the dispatch of food parcels containing Lamingtons, Vegemite sarnies and tubes of Foster's to assuage their longing for home comforts. Filled with relief that I had coped so admirably and congratulating myself on a job well done, I picked up my knitting – I was making a long striped Dr Who-type scarf for cycling in – and spun round in my swivel chair to scan

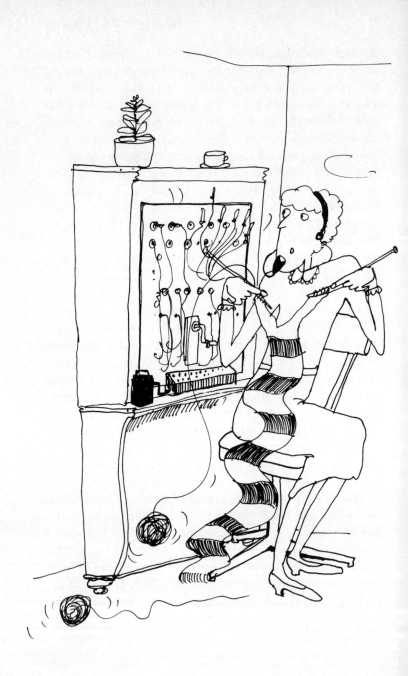

the entrance hall. With wicked accuracy, the long knitting needle threaded itself behind all the phone cords, and with one effortless jerk, powered by my swing, pulled every single one out. At one stroke the whole bunch were disconnected. It was another hour before they were all retrieved and reconnected, and in the process I was on the receiving end of a lot of picturesque Aussie vituperation; some of it was even more colourful than my scarf.

That was my finest hour, my zenith of ineptitude. In fact, with practice I did get a bit better at it, and sometimes as much as a whole morning passed without my making more than a couple of bodges. Some guests were, naturally, more trouble than others, constantly ringing down with enquiries and orders as well as placing endless calls, and one of the worst offenders was a popular and well-known comedian – star of stage, screen and radio, as they say – who was appearing in pantomime in the nearby city. Unlike most funny men who, mercifully, are only funny on stage, this one was a 24-hours-a-day joker, ringing down from his suite with messages and requests which he obviously thought hilarious but drove us to distraction. He got at us all – the chambermaids, the bell-boys whom he sent on pointless errands, and even that pillar of the establishment and fount of all knowledge, the head porter. Ours was called Patrick, and it didn't pay to upset him; for he was a man with connections. Given sufficient monetary encouragement, Patrick could, and would, provide a splendidly wide range of services, from a hot tip for the 2.45 at Newbury, through theatre seats for a fully-booked show, to the acquisition of a lady highly skilled in the ancient arts of reviving tired businessmen. Laughing Boy did not, in Patrick's opinion, accord him the respect to which he was entitled; but, like the rest of us, he bore it with gritted teeth and a tight smile in expectation of a handsome gesture of appreciation when the jolly japer finally departed. Laughing Boy was well-heeled, having been established at the top of his particular tree for a very long time. A large tip was happily anticipated by all.

At last the panto season drew to a close, and the day of departure arrived. His luggage, flashily monogrammed, lay in the reception hall. His Rolls was due at the front door at any moment. The little dolls' eyes belonging to the telephone in his suite summoned me lasciviously for what I fervently hoped was the last time, and his dresser imparted the thrilling news that Laughing Boy himself was on his way down in the lift to distribute tokens of appreciation. Excitement ran high; the bell-boys formed a chorus-line and practised holding out their palms, Patrick stood loftily aloof by the revolving door, practising his famed sleight of hand, and I leaned over my counter and practised a blindingly grateful smile whilst mentally planning how to spend my tip. Something for the children, I thought: boots for my daughter? new running spikes for my son? There might even, I conjectured optimistically, be enough for both. Heaven knows I'd spent enough time and effort taking and passing on messages, contacting agents, ringing costumiers, arranging assignations, making and cancelling appointments and laughing dutifully at the tenth as well as the first telling of a joke.

The lift purred to a halt and we all sprang to attention. The doors whispered open, and Laughing Boy stepped into the ankle-deep carpets. He was carrying a large cardboard carton. Goodness, he must be planning to fling bank notes all over the place! Grinning, he approached the line of bell-hops and began to distribute the largesse. His back was towards me, so all I could see were the boys' faces as he passed along the line, pressing something into each outstretched hand. They bore the stunned look of one who has been hit smartly and unexpectedly over the head with a brick. Then it was my turn. He came over and, with a merry quip, handed me my gratuity, pressing it into my palm with an unnecessary amount of hand-holding. As soon as he let go, I looked down. I had been right in thinking this would be something for the children. But not boots; not running shoes. What he had bestowed on each one of us was a quarter-pound bag of pink and white marshmallows.

It was just as well that we were all struck dumb. The Rolls was safely out of earshot before Patrick exploded. And I must say, I couldn't have put it better myself.

Not all the guests had such a warped sense of humour, nor such a tight hold on their wallets. Sometimes, especially when I took private dictation from foreign businessmen, the tips were gratifyingly generous. Being in a position of high dignity, Venetia could not, of course, act as secretary to the guests; but I, being a mere part-time menial, could. It had some disadvantages – a few of the gentlemen expected rather more than shorthand and had to be rapidly disillusioned as to my duties – but on the whole they took my diplomatic evasions well and only once did I have to threaten to send for my three Knights. The tips came in very handy – indeed, I almost relied on them – five shillings an hour didn't exactly amount to a king's ransom, especially part-time. Many's the day I laboured on at the typewriter, eyelids drooping with weariness and fingers seizing up with cramp, for another half-hour's overtime; the precious half-crown it yielded was badly needed.

Venetia, even if she could have lowered herself, had no need of either tips or overtime. I never discovered what her salary was but it was certainly lavish compared to mine, and what with having her meals provided and living in, she couldn't have had much to spend it on, either.

Her great extravagance was clothes. She bought all her accoutrements in London, and none of your cut-rate tat, either; her well-cut tent-coats and enormous dresses bore exclusive labels. It was the same with her shoes. A lot of larger ladies have surprisingly pretty ankles and feet; Venetia was not one of them. She had legs like traffic bollards and feet as broad as they were long; a sunny barefoot childhood in South Africa had spread them like blocks of Wensleydale. Like one of the Ugly Sisters, she crammed them into beautiful creations from Regent Street and Bond Street, creations with delicate straps and low-cut fronts; her ankles would billow above them, and her toes seemed constantly to be trying to escape, bursting out through the thongs like button mushrooms seeking the light. She would ease her shoes off under her desk with little moans of relief, unable to resist the pleasure of unleashing her feet even though it meant going through all the agony of imprisoning them again as soon as she had to stand up.

Once, having watched this painful performance several times in one morning, I ventured to ask her, over our coffee and biscuits, why she always chose such frivolous footwear; surely it would have been more comfortable to wear something flatter, less strappy, more roomy? 'Yis, I wish I could reely,' she said in a tone which, in someone more feminine, could have been construed as a mixture of wistfulness and pride, 'but it's my friend, you see. My *man* friend. He likes a dainty shoe.' Venetia? With a *man* friend? The mind went into over-boggle. I *had* to know more.

'A man friend?' I probed delicately, retrieving my eyebrows and trying to envisage a man brave enough, and big enough, to tackle Venetia. She positively bridled – a sight calculated to make strong men blench – and confessed that, yes, she had an admirer, whom she had met in London on one of her frequent clothes-shopping trips. Tactfully I refrained from asking how and where, but she seemed suddenly eager to unburden herself, to confide in another woman, even one as humble as I. She certainly didn't have any female friends that I knew of, and her longing to talk about her conquest had obviously overcome her sense of superiority.

She had, she told me almost shyly, met him in Hyde Park – at Speakers' Corner, where he had been addressing a small uninterested group on the evils of apartheid. Venetia, catching the drift of his harangue as she passed on her way to the Ritz (where she planned to treat herself to afternoon tea), had been sufficiently roused to engage him in public debate. My admiration for the man increased; Venetia aroused was a formidable force, as I knew to my cost. The debate had become heated, and had sunk fairly rapidly to mere argument, and thence swiftly into the sort of row so beloved of the true Speakers' Corner habitué. Lord Soper's audience deserted him. The forecasters of doom and disaster of various kinds found themselves addressing the empty air. Only pigeons and the occasional squirrel listened to those advocating the breakup of the EEC, Rights for Single Yellow Gay Fathers, or total abstinence as a cure for all mankind's ills. Everyone was gathered round Venetia and her adversary, heckling, egging on and waiting hopefully for the first blow to be struck.

In this, at least, they were disappointed. Venetia had too much sense of dignity to stoop so low. Instead, realising suddenly that (a) she was a centre of attention and (b) she was losing the argument, she swung ponderously on her heel like the *Queen Elizabeth* at anchor, and with a final recommendation that the speaker should get his knees brown before tackling a subject of which he had no experience, she pushed through the crowd and sailed majestically off towards Marble Arch, too incensed even to be aware of the sound of footsteps hurrying behind her. She felt her arm seized and, thinking it was probably a bag-snatcher, turned with every intention of laying him out cold; however, she was astonished to see her erstwhile opponent. He had, he announced somewhat breathlessly, so much enjoyed their exchange; it was so rare, he went on, to find a woman of spirit, a real woman, prepared to stand up for her beliefs. No matter, he added, how misguided those beliefs might be. Would she, perhaps, do him the honour of taking tea with him? Venetia had been so taken aback that she had let him get away with the bit about being misguided, and they ended up taking tea, cucumber sandwiches and iced fancies at the Ritz together.

That had been the start of something big – how could it be anything else? – the start of what appeared to be a meeting of twin souls. Passion had been kindled over the teacups, and their relationship had, since then, reached heights of intimacy hitherto unknown to Venetia. My respect for this Samson of the soapbox grew with every revelation; and I was dying to know what he looked like. I was just about to ask when Venetia delved into her Gucci handbag and extracted a photograph. 'That's him,' she said fondly, 'that's my Victor.' What an appropriate name, I thought – the man deserves a crown of laurels, a niche in the Hall of Fame. I hardly dared look at the photo, I was so afraid that he would turn out to be the complete opposite of Venetia – a small and skinny Jack Sprat to her Jack Sprat's Wife.

But he wasn't – he was gigantic. There was no other word for it. He stood a good six and a half feet tall, was extremely burly – twenty stone, at a guess – and heavily bearded into the bargain. He resembled a heavyweight wrestler in top condition. But then, I reasoned, he'd need to be. 'He calls me his little flower,' confided Venetia, and her face looked quite different; it was softened and more rounded, like a boulder after several centuries under running water. I was astounded by this new vision of her; it was so difficult to picture Venetia in the throes of passion.

'Where do you, er, *meet*?' I managed, suppressing my desire to giggle with tremendous effort. 'There's a small hotel,' she said, lowering her voice confidentially. 'With a wishing well?' – my imagination was getting out of hand now, and I hurriedly had to pretend to blow my nose to retain control.

'We take a room for the afternoon,' she murmured, 'but no one suspects what for, because I always take my own sheets. And sometimes,' and here she really and truly blushed, 'we do it in the bath.'

To this day I still hope Venetia believed my explanation that it was an errant biscuit crumb which forced me to rush, choking, from the room.

Even these new aspects of Venetia, combined with the delights of my three Knights of the Holey Overalls, were not enough, however, to tempt me into staying in the job permanently. For one thing the wages were too low for comfort, and for another I was spreading in all directions due to an unremitting diet of fried everything. It had got beyond the stage where cycling could cope with it, and I could foresee a time in the not-too-distant future when Venetia and I would look like Tweedledum and Tweedledee. I couldn't face life in a series of ever-larger tents, and neither could I forgo the fried bread. There was only one solution: I'd have to find another, less fattening,

job and leave the hotel. So I did, after a final farewell nosh-up in the staff kitchen at which I was treated to approximately a million calories, give or take a few, and presented with my very own tea mug. It was a touching occasion, and made up for the fact that I never did manage to mingle with the rich and famous. Unless you count

Laughing Boy. Although, come to think of it, I did once catch a glimpse of Bing Crosby's left ear, as he went out through the revolving doors; it was a very pretty pink, with the sun shining through it.

Temp-ting Offers

So, I hoped the Belfast temp agency wouldn't find me a job in a hotel: I don't think I'm temperamentally suited to it, what with all that food lying around, not to mention the temptation to nip into the bar at lunchtime for a quick one to set you up for the afternoon. Fighting to keep your eyes open over the typewriter afterwards, it just isn't worth it. I took the obligatory typing test – no trouble at all, whiz whiz clatter clatter, ping, fingers a blur over the keys – and the shorthand test – thank heavens for a good memory – gave the interviewer a carefully edited curriculum vitae, and filled in the necessary forms. I wasn't fussy, I told the woman; all I asked was a not-too-demanding job in pleasant surroundings, for a nice boss, at a good wage. She raised her eyes heavenwards. 'Don't we all?' she sighed, doubtless echoed in spirit by all secretaries throughout the land. But she did the best she could; a typing job with a building society, for a whole fortnight. The wage wasn't exactly going to turn Jackie Onassis green with envy, but at least I'd be paying my way and buying my own tights. And it gave me an excuse not to do any more housework – not that I've ever needed an excuse. What's the point of doing something that's only going to need doing all over again tomorrow?

My first day at the building society was lovely; I think I typed about one letter, and spent the rest of the time chatting. The girls were very friendly and, as they say in

Ulster, the crack was great; they were amused and horrified, in equal parts, that I could even contemplate leaving
the lights of London for the uncertainties of Belfast. They
still thought of London as being the swinging city of the
Sixties, with its streets paved, if not with gold, at least
with primroses. Most of them longed to go there, but
hardly any of them thought they ever really would. 'I
couldn't leave the mammy,' was the usual excuse. It was
my first encounter with the close Ulster family ties, where
many girls, on marriage, still only move round the corner
from the mammy and many men marry late, if at all,
because they live at home, are bound to ageing parents,
and see no need for independence.

It's almost unheard of for children to leave home *before*
they marry, unless it's to go to college or university. When
I told them that both mine had left home at seventeen to
strike out on their own, never to return as permanent
residents, the girls looked at me decidedly askance. Here,
obviously, their accusing eyes said, was a cruel and selfish
mother, turfing her children out of the nest while they
were still wet behind the ears; unnatural, they thought it,
and asked me if I hadn't been terribly upset about their
leaving. Not apart from missing their company and hoping
they'd choose their new company carefully, I said; after
all, they had to learn to look after themselves sometime,
and the sooner the better. Also, I pointed out, perhaps
tactlessly, it meant that their parents were able to live
their own life, too. 'But your children *are* your life!' I was
told in shocked tones – what more, they implied, could a
woman ask than a lifetime of serving her family?

I immediately felt laden with guilt, convinced that I had
condemned my luckless offspring to a hopeless future,
warped by the knowledge that their mother didn't love
them and had got rid of them at the first opportunity in

41

order to lead a life of profligate, irresponsible carousing. 'I wrote to them,' I protested apologetically, 'every week, and did their laundry when they came home for weekends.' Stacks of laundry, all the same indeterminate shade of launderette grey, plus disgusting, long-hoarded sports kits. Surely that counted for something? Not, it seemed, in Belfast. I should have insisted on their staying at home, done their washing, cleaned their rooms, made their beds, censored their mail, vetted their friends, mended their clothes, worn myself to a frazzle living for and through them and then launched them into their own little world of marriage, totally inexperienced in looking after themselves, let alone anyone else. I stopped feeling guilty and felt glad that my son could turn out a magnificent curry and iron his own shirts, and my daughter could make her own clothes and hang paper. I couldn't do any of those things when I first married. I still can't.

Once the other girls had accepted that I wasn't really intrinsically evil, but merely odd because I was English, they stopped worrying about my shortcomings as a parent and were very friendly and helpful indeed. They escorted me to the shops at lunchtime so that I learned my way around the city centre, and showed me the right way to go through the security gates. (The first time I'd been in town on my own, I'd walked innocently along the road instead of presenting myself at the hut for searching, and had suffered the indignity of being yelled at by a lady security officer, who had summoned me back and searched me crossly before letting me proceed, guaranteed free of bombs and other undesirable objects.) The girls explained which doors in the big stores were for going in, to pass the man with the instrument like an electronic kettle-element which buzzed if you had something forbidden about your person, and which doors were for going out again. It all took time, and practice. If there was a queue at the ingoing door, you couldn't barge gaily in through another; they were all locked.

As well as providing me with all this essential information, they also introduced me, more happily, to the delicious buns of Belfast – where all small cakes are buns – and to the multitude of different breads. Wheaten farls, potato bread, soda bread, wheaten soda, barmbrack – all irresistible. And all packed with calories. But not so packed as the Pavlovas, for which every Ulster housewife has her secret recipe; I'd thought that these glorious confections, huge nests of meringue crispy without, melting within, stuffed with fruit and crowned with whipped cream, were peculiar to Australia. I was delighted to make their acquaintance in the little café opposite the building society, where 'a wee slice of Pavlova' with your coffee turned out to be about five inches high, three inches wide and absolutely guaranteed to send you back across the road totally sated. It's just as well I was only there for such a short time; my waistline would never have recovered. It threatened to be like the Cotswold hotel all over again. There's one thing you can say for my jobs: they may not be well paid, but by God they're nourishing.

In two weeks I put on half a stone, learned where all the best 'buns' in Belfast could be found and made a complete hash of operating the office teleprinter, the mysteries of which became more and more profound the harder I tried to penetrate them. In the end the manager wouldn't let me anywhere near it, which suited me fine. We said fond farewells when the fortnight was up, although the manager offered me a permanent position which, in the interests of my figure, I turned down, and it was on to the next temporary placement. I missed them though, especially the Pavlovas.

* * *

'The Meat Marketing Board needs a temp,' the girl from the agency told me over the phone, 'they want a shorthorn typist.' No, it wasn't the pun I took it for, just the Belfast accent, but the idea tickled me and I needed the money, so I trotted off to the address she gave me. It turned out to be a small neat office not far from the flat – lovely, that meant another twenty minutes in the sack every morning followed by a mere three-minute panic-stricken run to get to work on time. It was the cosy, informal sort of establishment where knitting is fished out of desks at slack moments, and there were very few visitors. Just my style.

In addition to taking down shorthorn, deciphering it – never easy – and typing it up, I also had to take a turn on the switchboard, which proved to be unexpectedly complicated. Not the actual mechanics of the thing – after the Cotswold hotel experience it was a miracle of modern science – but interpreting the messages that came through. Every afternoon, when everyone else had gone home and I was alone in the office, farmers from all over the province would ring in with the day's fatstock prices. This was bad enough – the terminology might as well have been Greek as far as I was concerned. But it was the country accents that really confounded me. My ear was slowly becoming attuned to the Belfast accent, but now I was bombarded, over a crackly telephone line, with voices from Ballymena, Derry, and all points north, south, east and west. It was worse than Greek; I couldn't even pick out the occasional familiar word, and taking down the reports took ages because I had to ask for everything to be spelt out. Goodness knows what happened to the fatstock prices during that fortnight. It's a wonder the bottom didn't fall out of the market. I got some super free recipe leaflets, though, even if I couldn't afford the meat to use them: I wish someone had tipped me with a couple of pounds of prime steak.

After that came a stint in a solicitor's office, where I dealt with the most fascinating letters and found out some of the dire tricks people can pull on one another under the strain of divorce or the prospect of gain. There was a fortnight at a chartered accountant's, typing endless balance sheets and getting right down to the end of the last column before I spotted the error in the first. Next, a week – which was quite long enough – in a commercial concern where the office supervisor took her duties so seriously that she timed each letter typed and handed out the stationery with all the open-handed generosity of a Scrooge. Accustomed as I was to returning home with my shopping bag stuffed full of bodged letters, ruined stencils and spoiled reports, so that my office wastepaper basket couldn't be held against me, I found this a dreadful strain. The wretched woman actually counted out the minimum number of sheets necessary for each job, like a French lavatory attendant, and woe betide you if you had to ask for more. I had to all the time, of course, and was betided by a lot of woe throughout the week. 'Not *another* sheet?' she would snarl at me, as I stood in front of her desk beseechingly. 'I gave you *more than enough* to finish that letter. What d'you do with it, eat it?' Resisting the temptation to tell her what I'd prefer to do with it, I would stammer out some excuse about spilt coffee or accidental tearing. I dare not tell her I'd started off with 'Deaf Madman' or 'Dead Sor' because my fingers had somehow alighted on the wrong keys. It was awful. I felt as if I were in some sort of Nazi kindergarten, and it was a great relief when the last afternoon finally arrived. I regret to tell you that I blew her a very rude raspberry indeed as I passed her desk on my way out.

After that there was a frightening period when no work at all came in. It seemed that no one needed a temp for anything; presumably all the resident staff had finished taking their holidays and all vacant positions had been permanently filled. It was the first time in my life that I'd been out of work when I wanted to be in. I'd have done any job: charing, office cleaning, shop assistant, bus conductress, street sweeper, brain surgeon, anything. But nothing was forthcoming. I was either too qualified or not qualified enough. The loss of independence was awful. I decided to go and throw myself on the tender mercies of the social services; surely they wouldn't leave me to face the world penniless?

Dressed to impress, in what I hoped was shabby gentility, and with laddered tights – to tug at the heart-strings of officialdom – I arrived at the local offices and took my place in a queue that seemed a mile long. We shuffled slowly into the main office and took our places on the benches; the whole building was sordid and cheerless. Next to me a group of men sat in a fog of cigarette smoke, discussing their newest acquisitions in the field of video and hi-fi. Can't be too bad, I thought hopefully, if they can rise to that sort of thing; the only form of music-player I had was so old that it was still called a gramophone and had to be wound up. At last my name was called, and I found myself face to face in the little unprivate cubicle with a tiny girl who looked as if she'd only left school that week. Unfortunately she couldn't see the laddered tights; or if she did, her heart-strings remained untugged. A great many questions later, it transpired that I wasn't after all eligible for any help, because (a) I had made the wrong decision years ago and opted to pay the Married Women's stamp – a false economy – and (b) I was Living with a Man. Useless to point out that I didn't want Himself to support me, useless to argue that I wanted to pay my own way. I was Living with a Man, and bureaucracy assumed, in its quaint old-fashioned way, that he was keeping me in the manner to which I was accustomed. I had been too honest; I should have told them I was merely lodging with Himself, paying rent, being a friendly tenant.

I'd have to hurry up and find some sort of work soon, or I could see myself having to leave Himself and move into a place of my own so that I could be eligible for assistance. On second thoughts, that was too great a sacrifice; we'd have to learn to live on one not-very-large wage instead of two, until I could con someone into employing me again . . .

Meanwhile, back at the ranch, things were progressing very satisfactorily. The flat, having been rigorously scoured during my first week in residence, was now lying fallow, building up a nice homely patina of light protective dust which would take at least a year to build up to the original depth. Seized with unwise enthusiasm one night, I had scraped all the paint off the sitting-room door in the hope of finding beautiful pine underneath. It had turned out to be old tea chests under all the layers and not worth the trouble, so after a few weeks of living with a leprous door we bought a cut-price can of canary yellow gloss and went mad with it, painting not only the door but everything that didn't actually dodge when it saw you approaching with the paintbrush. It cheered things up no end, even if we did have to wear sunglasses in the bath.

But the real fly in the ointment was the spare bedroom, with its piles of junk that defied penetration and its skylight locked tight with the spiders' webs of years. Worst of all, there were Funny Noises in there at night. When Himself was out, I could hear little pattering noises, and once or twice a scratching sound. I lay in bed and prayed, oh don't let it be rats . . .

It wasn't rats. It was dear little mice, doubtless relations of the ones who had made the hole in the kitchen wainscoting. I hated the thought of putting down traps – what if a mouse was caught by the leg and had to be dispatched? What if I trod on a trap in my bare feet while I was unearthing something? The only answer was to invest in a cat.

The local paper had advert after advert of kittens seeking good homes with light mousework; but without transport, most of them were too far away to go and see. I fancied a half-Siamese, the kind which had ruled my past life so effectively with a paw of iron. Ulster Siamese-cat owners, however, seemed to keep their queens under more rigid purr-dah than the English. Not a half-Siamese was to be found: it was a full-blooded one at an astronomical price, or nothing. I was seized with the old familiar cat-yearning. I had to have a kitten, and *fast*. I began casting covetous glances at passing felines, and contemplating catnap. Before I was driven to snatching one, however, Himself came home one day and announced that one of his workmates had a spare kitten looking for a home. Problem solved! Or so we thought. . .

A couple of days later Lucy arrived, a tiny scrap of a grey creature rattling about in a cardboard box. We opened the lid and Lucy leapt out and went to earth instantly under the sofa. Ten minutes, two crumpled paper balls and a bitten hand later, I had her out and crouched in my hands, trembling and growling; she was petrified. How were we to know that poor Lucy was half-wild, a farm kitten, who had never in her short life been inside a house before? No wonder she was in a state. She hated being stroked, she was frightened by everything, and she had no idea about using a sand tray. Because she was so nervous we put her into the spare room with food and a tray, and left her quietly alone to get her bearings, and the odd mouse if possible. But it didn't work. She just hid under the debris as soon as the door was opened, refusing to come out, impervious to coaxing and comforting. We tried her in the kitchen; she took a flying leap on to the top of the hot stove and walked through the frying pan,

scattering food as she went. She stood up on her hind legs in corners, like a little rearing horse, and made messes. She retreated under the dresser and cried. It was heartbreaking. We stood it for four days and then, sadly, I put her back into the cardboard box and sent her home to her mother. She had purred once for me, a tiny rusty little sound. Back on the farm, she settled down immediately in her familiar yard and eventually became a first-class mouser: our mice continued to flourish unabated.

At least they weren't rats. But even rats are not without a certain charm – although I doubt whether there will ever be another with the charisma of Fred. Fred was a rat in a million. I met him in Berkshire.

After the Cotswold hotel caper, I took a part-time job as secretary and assistant to an experimental psychologist. The work promised to be interesting and unusual; part of it was the setting up and running of experiments on visual and aural comprehension and retention. (I hoped that at last I might find out the root cause of my own affliction of instant forgettery – my short-term memory seemed to last all of several seconds.) Arriving at the laboratory on the first morning, I had no sooner arrived in the entrance hall than I made Fred's acquaintance. He was waiting at Reception, sitting up on the desk washing himself with great application and immense aplomb, considering that he had a little electrode protruding from the top of his head.

RECEPTION

It gave him the outlandish appearance of a small visitor from another planet; I wouldn't have been at all surprised if he had demanded to be taken to my leader. The two cleaning ladies pinned against the wall on the other side of the desk were not nearly so full of confidence; they half-heartedly brandished defensive mops, but Fred kept them at bay easily by simply dropping on to all fours and advancing a soft step towards them. When they shrank back, he sat upright again and resumed his toilet. He was pink and white (and silver, if you counted the electrode), and immaculately clean; he was really very pretty. For a rat, that is.

The ladies seemed very relieved to see me. Presumably they thought there was safety in numbers, or perhaps they expected me to grab hold of the Beast of Berkshire and somehow dispose of him. Momentarily distracted by my arrival, he took his eye off the cleaners, who immediately became unhypnotised and seized the opportunity to hurry over to join me at a safe distance from the desk. 'Escaped from the lab, he has,' panted the stouter of the two. ' 'Orrible creature, give you the creeps, bite you as soon as look at you, like as not.' 'Probably go straight for the throat,' I agreed comfortingly, admiring Fred's gleaming white teeth as he nibbled at a recalcitrant bit of something on his tummy. 'Inny *awful*,' shuddered the second lady. 'Int natural, is it? Them things in their 'eads, I mean.' They stood behind me and peered cautiously at the menace, who was now washing his feet intently. We stood for a minute or two and watched each other. He certainly didn't look very savage, and although rats come fairly low down on my list of favourite animals I felt I could take to Fred.

I made a tentative step forward, wondering if I might be able to bag him with a waste-paper basket before he got away. But before I could make a move, a figure in a white coat came rushing down the stairs, uttering loud cries of relief. 'Fred! Thank goodness you've found Fred!' he gasped, swooping down on the desk like a mother homing-pigeon. Fred sat up, with his pink nose whiffling, and uttered several squeaks of what sounded like greeting. The lab technician picked him up, to the accompaniment of shrieks of disgust from the cleaners, and cuddled him up against his shoulder fondly. 'He got out when the cages were being cleaned,' he explained, as Fred explored his ear. 'I've been looking *everywhere* – I was afraid he might get lost. Very fond of Fred we all are,' he went on, turning the creature over on its back in his arms and doing a spot of tummy-tickling. 'Very bright, Fred. Learns in a flash, you don't catch him pressing the wrong levers.'

All this was Chinese to me, of course. Why did Fred have to press levers? Was there a small manufacturing business going on upstairs somewhere, turning out some sort of product – ratchets? – which required lever-pulling and button-pressing? Whatever it was, Fred looked not only amazingly fit and healthy but quite happy in his work, too. I hoped they paid him the right wages, with extra for overtime; perhaps he belonged to some organisation like ALARM – Association of Laboratory Animals and Rat Mechanics – in which no doubt he would occupy the position of shop-steward. The technician – who introduced himself, now that the panic was over, as Jim – held Fred out towards us. 'He's very tame,' he said. 'Would you like to hold him?' The two cleaners, overcome at the very thought, fled giggling and screaming through a nearby door, clanking their mops and buckets behind them. I thought Fred looked very sweet, despite the teeth, and I'd never held a rat before – I'd never *seen* a rat before – so I accepted the offer. Fred was handed over;

he was surprisingly heavy, and leaned against my shoulder as nicely as could be, nuzzling my neck and making his little squeaky noises. 'There,' exclaimed Jim, beaming fondly, 'he's taken to you. Come on, we'll go back upstairs and you can see him at work.'

I didn't need a second invitation – it's not every day you get the chance to see a rodent shop-steward in action – and we laboured up two flights of stairs with Fred getting heavier and more affectionate at every step. He was by now busily engaged in trying to remove my earrings. I began to fear for my earlobes, but fortunately we reached our destination before he'd done more than remove one butterfly-clasp from the back of my ear and drop it neatly down the front of my blouse. Jim opened a door and ushered me and my burden into a large, sunny room. There was a budgie in a cage, hanging from the ceiling, and several more cages against the wall, all containing replicas of Fred. They all rushed to the front of their houses as soon as they saw us, standing up against the wire and hanging on with their little pink feet; one or two of them had antennae like Fred, but most were unadorned.

Rather to my disappointment, there was no sign of a miniature production line. Just the cages, the budgie and dozens of pot plants covering every level surface. There was a kettle and cups on a tray, too. I hoped Jim would offer me a cuppa – it had been a long bike ride to work, and the drama of Fred had made me even thirstier. Fortunately, the first thing Jim did was to fill the kettle and switch it on. 'I'll just set up the apparatus, and then Fred can show off for you,' he said and, leaving me still nursing his star performer, he bustled about with a glass case and various mysterious bits and pieces, only breaking off to brew a pot of extremely weak tea.

At last everything was ready, especially Fred, who

was getting into a fluster of excitement, whiffling and squeaking like mad and trying to scrabble out of my arms towards the glass case. Jim popped him in, and he immediately took up his position in front of several lights and three levers with the relaxed ease and confidence of the accomplished professional. I leaned against the desk, sipping the awful tea, and watched the proceedings. Jim operated buttons at the back of the case, the lights shone in certain sequences, and Fred went into action like a veteran. One red light and he pressed the left-hand lever, sitting up on his haunches with his paw on the handle. A pellet of food shot down a tube and Fred neatly fielded it in mid-air. Two lights shone – Fred moved to the centre lever, pressed it and darted to another tube just in time to imbibe a slug of flavoured water. Three lights – and like a flash he was in front of the third lever, which was set over a small metal grille, had it pressed down with the speed of lightning and then sat there motionless, with his eyes closed. I observed him anxiously. Had he missed his cue? Pressed the wrong lever? Fallen asleep on duty? Forgotten? Was his short-term memory as bad as mine? Or was he simply on strike?

Fred still didn't move, but I noticed his whiskers tremble briefly before he opened his eyes, shook himself, and trotted back to sit expectantly in front of the lights, all ready for the next task. 'What was he supposed to do then?' I asked, embarrassed for Fred that he had fluffed it in front of a stranger. 'Oh, that's his favourite sequence,' explained Jim. 'He'd have that one all the time if he had the choice. When three lights flash and he's sitting on that little grid, his pleasure centres are stimulated. He loves it.' That explained the antenna. I didn't like to enquire any more deeply into the workings of the machine, although I was longing to know how it worked and what 'pleasure centres' were involved. If it was what I thought it was, poor Fred. What a way to get your kicks. Although I must admit, he didn't seem to feel that he was missing out on anything: even while he was busily pressing levers for pellets or hooch, he kept gazing longingly towards the little metal grille. Whatever turns you on, I suppose. But also, beggars can't be choosers. And at least a glass cage never gets a headache.

Fred was a fitting introduction to the laboratory. The part of my job that I enjoyed most was helping to run the experiments – on human guinea pigs, I hasten to add, not real ones. They were fascinating, especially as I hadn't a clue as to what they were supposed to be designed to prove most of the time. As far as I could make out, as soon as one psychologist published a paper proving his theory beyond a shadow of contradiction, someone else immediately came up with their own theory proving the exact opposite. Still, it kept them happily occupied and they seemed harmless enough.

Running the tests was just like helping at the children's playgroup – guessing games with cards and shapes, and lots of flashing lights and visual displays. I loved it. I was plunged straight into my first experiment on my second day; the subject – a small bald male student no doubt in need of the pittance that would be his reward – had to sit in a darkened cubicle and report on a series of coloured lights which I had to project on to a screen. It was a pity he was such a scrawny unattractive type, really – there were several lab assistants and student psychologists with whom I wouldn't have minded being closeted in the dark – but it kept my mind on the job. This particular test, however, seemed to go wrong from the start. The poor lad consistently reported incorrect sequences and I began to fear for the outcome of the experiment. Perhaps, I thought worriedly, he needed glasses and wouldn't wear them for fear of blighting his appearance still further. But really, his results were appalling; out of about thirty sets of colours, he got less than half right.

At last the test was over and we both stumbled, half-blinded, out into the office. He departed clutching his meagre payment and I began to collate the results. Blimey O'Reilly, I thought, this is ridiculous, and decided to do something about it. I felt so sorry for the poor myopic student, and for my boss too; it seemed such a waste of time, trying to work with results like that, so I doctored them as carefully as I could to give the subject a more favourable score. It took me half an hour of concentrated thought. When I'd finished, I typed up the figures neatly, bunged them on to the boss's desk and departed, well satisfied, for home.

The following day I arrived at the usual hour and, opening the office door, was surprised to see my employer slumped across his desk. The light of desperation was in his eyes; all round him lay pieces of paper covered in figures, his hair was on end, his ashtray overflowed, he held a cup of black coffee in trembling hands. Directly in front of him was the typed list of yesterday's results. He raised his head and gazed haggardly at me through red-rimmed eyes.

'I can't understand it,' he whimpered. 'I must have gone completely wrong somewhere. I've been going over and over these figures all night. They were supposed to prove my theory finally and incontrovertibly, and somehow the whole thing's been turned on its head. I just can't understand it,' he repeated brokenly and, seizing a pencil, he began to do frantic calculations again. My heart sank into my red cycling socks. Tentatively, I enquired what

was wrong. A horrid suspicion was forming, and it proved to be dead right. The experiment had been to test the effects of colour-blindness.

It took more courage than I knew I had to confess; but my bravery paled into insignificance compared to the forgiveness and compassion displayed by my exhausted boss. Perhaps the relief of discovering that it wasn't he who was barmy was what did it. He merely closed his eyes, swallowed twice and asked in a voice rendered faint by iron self-control whether I had the original figures anywhere. They were still, thank heavens, in my waste-paper basket. If necessary, I'd have searched through every rubbish tip in town to find them. I was so grateful he hadn't sent me away to have a little electrode inserted in my brain.

After this inauspicious start I took terrible, painstaking care with test results, even when they struck me as totally daft, irrelevant, or misleading to the point where the only thing they seemed to prove was the old saying about there being lies, damned lies and statistics. I couldn't bear the guilt of maybe being responsible for my employer having a complete nervous breakdown and running amok through the laboratory. But I don't think he ever really trusted me completely again; I'd see him surreptitiously checking my waste-bin, smoothing out crumpled notes bearing such legends as '2 pot., btrt, cauli, loo p.', and I think he was quite relieved when my time there was up.

Baa Sinister

In our establishment, there are three recurrent total certainties. The first is that after any given night out on the town we will end up lovingly discussing the history, present condition and future prospects of the houseplants, even if only moments before we have – perhaps unwisely, considering our mature years – been swinging from the chandelier attempting to out-Sutra the Kama Sutra. The second is that the moment we sit down to a meal, the cat will, in a demonstration of her unequalled talent for feline naffery, put her sand tray to prolonged and extravagant use. And then there's the third: that, as surely as night follows day, as the bills come in so will Himself file them away and forget them.

He files them under the sofa, between books, on the hall table, in his bedside cupboard; in his sock drawer, on the bookcase, in the kitchen behind the tea caddy, on the attic floor. Anywhere. Everywhere. It isn't that he doesn't mean to pay them; he is completely willing if not always absolutely able. It's just that he quite simply doesn't regard them as a matter of any urgency. In his eyes, anything worth having is worth waiting for; he's waited a long time for the modest good things in his life to arrive and I suppose, in consequence, he feels that the Electricity Board, the television people, British Telecom and sundry other regular bill-senders share his philosophy. He'll pay them, given time – and think how much more they'll appreciate it, how pleased and excited they'll be when he finally does! And in the meantime, how about popping out for a modest Chinese dinner?

Conditioned as I was by a previous way of life wherein bills were paid practically before they hit the doormat, and imbued with a deep-seated Puritan fear of debt, I found the attitude very hard to take, let alone understand, at first. If the phone bill went unpaid for longer than two days after its arrival, I lived in dread of being cut off from contact with the civilised world; if the television rental wasn't settled by return of post I expected to get home from work to find the bailiffs kicking down the door.

Sifting through the invoices and trying to sort out the more urgent from those that could safely be postponed for another few weeks, I would suggest diffidently to my insouciant partner that maybe we might settle one or two of the more irate ones. Himself, ever willing to be agreeable, would select a few – the ones that stood out the most on account of the red stars and exclamation marks all over them – and write cheques to cover their demands, but I knew he was really quite sorry that the game had finally come to an end. Also, I suspected that in the back of his mind there lurked a faint but smouldering hope that if he could only manage to ignore them for long enough, they would go away. After a short but rigorous period of training it began to lurk in mine too, but without any degree of conviction; it was depressingly rarely fulfilled. Creditors as a species are very persistent. So the bills just went on dropping repetitiously through the letter box and Himself went on filing and forgetting them in all the old familiar nooks and crannies.

Certain payments due, however, never remained outstanding for long. Let the Electricity Board levy the charge of the light brigade, the coalman black us for debt, the television people plead with us to see our way clear – they could all take their turn in the monthly lottery, the blind shuffle of fate. But the club subs were inviolate, sacrosanct. Himself, having been a bachelor of the ungay sort for so long before meeting his nemesis, was deeply attached to his clubs and all they stood for – the comradeship, the old friends, the whole concept of all-boys-togetherness which seemed to me to consist in getting merrily full together and swopping jokes they'd all heard with monotonous regularity for the past twenty years. I used to wonder how they could still go on laughing at the fiftieth hearing, and came to the conclusion that it was a sort of conditioned reflex; I expect my psychologist ex-boss at the laboratory could have written a fascinating paper on it.

But Himself loves his clubs with a passionate fondness that would withstand any challenge. I've never dared to drive him to a choice between me and them – I'm not that sure of my powers of attraction. After all, decades of familiarity bind him with those chains of habit and affection that keep someone with their old unexciting partner despite the seductive temptations of a new love; the subs were paid, come hell or high water or mince for dinner five times in a week. After all, the clubs were there before I was, and it's amazing just how versatile mince can be if you put your mind to it. It's a good thing my imagination has always been the most fertile part of me.

The rugby club I had been introduced to on my first day in Belfast. The yacht club took longer, as the sailing season, thankfully short, was the only time of the year that Himself went down there. It was too far away for casual social visits, even if we'd had a car. When the late spring came, however, and with it the time for putting the boats into the water, I was initiated into the heady delights of the yacht club. Not, naturally, as a sailing member; my idea of yachting is to lie, bikinied, at the sharpish end of a fairly large and comfortable boat, imbibing chilled drinks and rotating gently under the rays of the sun like a chicken on a spit. Belfast sailing isn't exactly – or even remotely – like that; it's cold, wet, bumpy and expensive and it beats me why anyone ever wants to do it. But they do, with relentless enthusiasm and persistence, waddling out of the club house like multi-coloured Michelin men in their oilskins and boots to get frozen, sodden and exhausted before lurching back in again with their faces bright red, or pallid on the bad days, windblasted and salt-encrusted, to sink a very large amount of gin in a very short time. It was the middle bit – the actual sailing – that I was taken to watch. Himself installed me in a good position at the bay window, gave me a gin and bade me watch the racing.

I took a bracing swig of gin, choked slightly – it was an unexpected double, Himself must have been very keen for me to sit still, shut up and watch – and obediently fixed my gaze on the middle distance. Nothing exciting was visible, to me anyway. Just a lot of distant white sails pottering about apparently at random. After I'd asked when they were going to start and been told that they had, in fact, been locked in deadly combat for the past fifteen minutes, I sat for what seemed like hours in a fog of uncomprehending boredom, surrounded by knowledgeable nautical persons who all spoke a language that the stranger does not know.

'Hauling in the sheets' and 'going round the boys' sounded promising, but nothing happened; and they kept mentioning 'jibing', which I thought unnecessarily meanspirited of them. After all, *I* knew it was a daft pastime, but it seemed unkind for those who engaged in it to sneer at each other. 'Oh, a nice bit of tacking, James,' bayed the weathered sea dog at my side, taking a stiff pull at his pink gin. At last! Someone had said something I could understand. Anxious to make some – any – contribution to the conversation that would alleviate the impression that their old crewmate had burdened himself with a total idiot, I remarked brightly, 'Oh, is James's sail torn? How clever of him to mend it without stopping!' There was an awful silence.

Paling beneath his tan and avoiding the eyes of his peers, Himself suggested a nice little walk along the sea wall. Just the two of us. To his credit, I think he tried to smile as he hissed the invitation. Even more to his credit, he didn't push me in, and has even taken me back to the club from time to time. But nowadays I confine my conversation to strictly non-nautical matters.

Then, of course, there is the tennis club. Lest you should get the impression that I have allied myself to some sort of super-sportsman, a kind of Jack-of-all-games, let me make it clear that Himself doesn't actually play tennis. Or squash, or golf, or badminton, or, for the last few score years, rugby, even though his wallet bulges with membership cards as that of the upwardly-mobile with credit cards. He just loves to belong. It didn't take too much time before I too began my own little collection of cards, and for someone who had previously been distinctly unclubbable it made quite a change. My only previous experience of joining anything had been the Brownies, in which I sneakily enrolled every summer just before the annual outing, copping out again immediately afterwards before anyone could start going on about knots or needlework. But Himself considered that I ought to become a Lady Member of at least a couple of places, just to show willing and relieve him of the irksome burden of signing me in every time. And as it seemed my only chance of being any sort of a lady, even if only a courtesy one, I agreed.

I had hoped it might lead to jolly goings-on in the showers, or the opportunity to turn out as hooker for the fourths, but of course it didn't. It just means that I am privileged to carry my very own little front-gate key, which lies, virgin and untried, in my handbag. One of these days I will – I really will – turn up alone and christen my keys; but I'll lay even money that it will only be because Himself is already cosily ensconced in his time-honoured corner and has rung me up to say that 'the crack's great – turn the dinner off and come on down and join the party!' Until then, I'll just go on being that club cliché, that bête noire of the women's liberation movement, 'Old Whatsisname's wife', a sort of tolerated hanger-on. Though even that humble status is not without its compensations . . .

'Guess what?' Himself came bounding up the stairs, full of the relentless bonhomie of one who intends to regale his captive audience with a scintillating résumé of an evening spent putting the world to rights at the club bar.

'Mmmm?' I replied encouragingly from bed, where I was ensconced in my usual writing position, pad on knee, pen in hand. (I was mentally going through the alphabet in a frustrated attempt to find a rhyme for 'orange' and had got as far as 'porrinj'; I was wondering if I could get away with starting the next line with 'er'. On the pad was written, 'The sun was like a golden orange/Its rays reflected in the porrinj/er my mother gave to me.' It was *very* late, and I *was* tired.)

'Listen,' he cried, wrenching the pen from my fist and replacing it with a large vodka and water. He had my attention instantly. An unsolicited nightcap, at 1 am? Something *must* be up. It was. 'We're all going to Donegal for Easter!' he beamed. 'On the spur of the moment – the Monday Club, we're all going. And taking our wives,' he added magnanimously, as an afterthought. I must admit it *was* pretty exciting, once I'd got over the shock – it was two days before the Easter weekend, and I wasn't used to these last-minute decisions, but I'd never seen Donegal and was longing to go there. Clubs obviously had their good points; it was a lovely and unexpected surprise, the food I'd stockpiled for the holiday would keep in our newly acquired mini-fridge, and the thought of where the money was to come from to pay for it all never crossed my mind. I was learning. Take your opportunities while you may, and worry about the overdraft later.

So we went to Donegal. Everyone else had families to transport, which meant their cars were packed to the roof with offspring and the allied paraphernalia. Himself and I travelled with no responsibilities, by train and coach, leisurely if not exactly luxuriously; the countryside was beautiful, and we had plenty of time to admire it. Ulster is surprisingly pretty; the fields were full of wild daffodils and primroses, lambs skittered and leapt, foals made breakneck dashes round their dams before collapsing like camera stands. It was all very picturesque – a fact that was totally lost on the coach driver.

'On the left,' he intoned, 'youse will see the redundant airfield.' As a man, and woman, the occupants of the coach gazed obediently out at some totally featureless field. There was not even a windsock to mark the spot. We were passing through some of the prettiest, greenest, most Eastery landscape imaginable, and with unerring skill the driver persisted in drawing our attention to the least interesting sights – the really banal and most patently obvious. 'This here,' he would announce, as we passed a massive roadsign with two-feet-high lettering that only a blind man could have missed, 'is Letterkenny' (or Londonderry, or Ballymurphy, or whatever). 'If youse will all look to the right,' he would continue, with the air of one about to spring a tremendously exciting surprise, 'youse will see the new industrial estate.' Not for him the joys of rural springtime.

Once over the border into Donegal, things got even more romantic; everywhere had that air of unsophisticated innocence that I remember from the countryside of my childhood. Hens and cockerels scratched together in small yards, ducks and geese grazed the fields, and here and there a donkey snoozed, head leaning over the fence. It really is idyllic countryside for the visitor; hard, certainly, for the small farmer, with its thin layer of topsoil, but beautiful to look at and walk over and breathe in, uncommercialised, unpolluted, and with vast tracts of it still uninhabited except for the odd cottage or isolated farm, and unused except for the occasional peat-bog where the fuel is still cut out and carted for the domestic hearth, as well as for the commercial market.

We bounced along the country roads, stopping in the middle of nowhere from time to time to drop someone off or wait for someone trudging down a long lane to the bus stop. And then at last, just like childhood holidays again, the cry went up, 'There's the sea!' And there it was, vast and emerald green and cobalt blue, and edged by the magnificent beaches of Donegal – miles long, firm and clean, silver-sanded, superb. And totally empty. You won't find lovelier beaches anywhere in the world, and they're nearly always bare of people; find yourself a glorious stretch of sand, and anyone nearer than half a mile away is practically an intruder. I was very puzzled. Why wasn't the place crammed, where were the rows of sun-worshippers, lying like sausages on a grill, slowly rotating until they reached the desired shade? Himself said I'd soon find out.

But that was to be a treat for the following day, apparently. By the time we reached our hotel, it was evening, and we were *ravenous*. A couple of rounds of cheese-and-chutney sandwiches hadn't gone very far, and, heartened by Himself's tales of gargantuan Donegal dinners, I could hardly wait for the first one to materialise in front of me. We flung our bags into the bedroom and rushed to find out what delights awaited us. The dining room was closed. Never mind, perhaps they served dinner later? I buttonholed the desk-clerk-cum-waiter-cum-porter-cum-general dogsbody. 'When can we have dinner?' I asked anxiously, hoping he couldn't hear my stomach rumbling or would take it for thunder over the distant Donegal hills. He smiled gently. 'Sure we don't do dinners until the summer,' he said. 'No one wants them – it would be a waste, so it would.' Seeing my face, he took pity. 'There's hamburgers in the bar, now,' he offered. 'Perhaps you'd take one of those. Or,' he continued, 'you could go up to the big hotel and get dinner there. It's just a wee dander up the road.' I knew what a wee dander it was – an Irish mile if ever there was one. I couldn't face it. So it was a hamburger in the bar, or nothing.

Once we were outside a couple of hamburgers each, we felt considerably better as to stomachs but the long day was catching up with us. The other members of the expedition were all staying up at 'the big hotel'; it was a bit more sophisticated – I mean, it even served *dinners* – and correspondingly more expensive. We'd made a tentative sort of arrangement to join them for a few welcoming beverages, but although the spirit was willing, the flesh was awfully weak. 'I know,' said Himself, 'let's take a quick lie-down, just a half-hour, before we go up there; it'll give us strength for the walk.' What a great idea, I thought. We shook our shoes off and fell on to bed. The next time I opened my eyes, it was pitch dark. I lit a match and peered at my watch. It was half-past two in the morning, and I had raging indigestion.

Breakfast in the morning more than made up for the privations of the previous night. We gorged on sausages, bacon, eggs, fried soda bread, black pudding, fried wheaten bread, toast, butter, marmalade and about two gallons of dark-brown tea, and waddled out, sated, into the sunshine. It was one of those rare days when Donegal could have been mistaken for the Mediterranean – the sea had the colour and richness of Greece, the sun shone, there wasn't a cloud in the sky. I could hardly wait to get on to that fabulous beach. 'Last one in the water's a cissy!' I yelled, pelting over the hard sand and rushing into the water. Up to my ankles. I couldn't go any further, because my feet had turned to stone. Blue stone. I was anchored to the spot with cold. It was exactly like bathing in ice cubes. The mystery of the empty beaches was solved; you'd need a centrally-heated, thermal, fur-lined dry-suit to bathe there. Himself, laughing callously, rescued me and rubbed my poor little frozen extremities until I could walk again unaided. 'Now you know,' he chuckled heartlessly. 'Fancy a spot of surfing?' If I'd been able to hobble a bit faster, I'd have pushed him in. As it was, I was absolutely delighted when a seagull, showing great perspicacity and unerring aim, made a direct and very messy hit on Himself, from a great height. It made me feel much better.

The next day was the last, and as a special treat Himself decided that I should have the enormous pleasure of accompanying him on a climb up Sheep's Head, a

deceptively gentle headland jutting out into the ocean. 'It's not much of a climb,' he assured me a bit patronisingly, 'you'll easily be able to manage it.' My blood was up. Manage it? Me, who had walked the hills of Africa – admittedly fifteen years ago, but still – of course I'd manage it. It looked gentle, and green, and inviting. I'd be up it like a rat up a drainpipe. I put on my track shoes, dungarees and a heavy sweater, and set off lightheartedly, a song on my lips and confidence in my heart.

Half an hour later, up to my knees in sticky bog,

lathered in perspiration and convinced my knees were broken, my confidence was ebbing fast. Infuriatingly Himself loped along in front of me, choosing footholds which didn't sink, keeping his feet dry, not even breathing hard. Every time I thought that surely we'd reached the final ridge, another one loomed up in front of us – they seemed to go on for ever. A mist came down. I got wetter. My left shoe came off in a morass and had to be extricated. By me, naturally; Himself was practically out of sight. Cursing, I battled on. Why wasn't I sitting with the other wives in a nice warm bar, knocking back the national beverage and waiting for the next meal to arrive? What on earth made me think I could keep up with a dedicated hill-climber who was in training? What the hell was I doing stuck up a damp God-forsaken mountain in the middle of nowhere, in the mist? Surely, at my age, I ought to have more sense . . .

Just as I was about to sink to my broken knees and give up the ghost, the mist vanished, the sun shone brilliantly, and it really was the last ridge! There was the cairn on top of the mountain, there was the unbroken view to the blue horizon, there was Himself sitting puffing his pipe, looking all fit and healthy and disgustingly unexhausted. I made it to the cairn and collapsed. It was bliss . . . the sun beat down on my battered body and it was soon so warm that I discarded the heavy sweater. Then the shirt. I was probably the first topless climber that Sheep's Head had ever experienced. We ate our sandwiches and drank our beer and basked, and it was all worth the agony. I put my shirt back on eventually and we started the descent. It *had* to be easier than going up, or so I hoped.

And it was, up to a point. At least, different muscles were being tortured, and at times one could leap from one bit to another. I was doing this, thinking what fun it must be to be a mountain sheep leaping from crag to crag, when I came face to face with something that changed my mind about the joys of mountain sheepdom. Because there, hanging from a broken fence post and looking for all the world like some primitive totem, was a ram's skull, complete with curled horns. It was stripped clean by the rain and sun, and through the eye-sockets was looped a length of wire. It hung there and rocked gently in the breeze. How had it got there? How had the ram died? Why was the wire threaded through the eyes? I didn't like to think too closely about that. But I knew he was an omen, and a good one, and I had to take him with me. So I carefully untangled him from the post, and wrapped him in our lunchbag. We decided he was definitely someone who should join our assorted household *lares et penates*, and that his name was Baa Sinister. With him stashed in my rucksack, we carried on down the mountain.

We were halfway down, almost within sight of level ground, when I discovered I'd left my heavy sweater on the cairn. 'I've left my jersey,' I wailed girlishly, sitting down thankfully and looking back at the looming mountain side. 'Silly girl, you,' said Himself, flinging himself backwards in a perfect Flying Angel into the thick, bouncy bracken. 'I'll wait for you here.' I hurled the rucksack and Baa Sinister at him and toiled off into the mountain fastnesses again. By the time I got back, wet through again, breathless, hot and cross, he was sleeping contentedly in the sun. I kicked him, none too gently, to wake him up, and he stretched happily. 'Get it all right?' he asked. 'That was a nice little snooze. Just what I needed.' I didn't speak to him for a full mile and a half. Sometimes he takes my peptalks about equality for women too far. He ought to be more selective.

* * *

As we sat in the train the next day, waiting for it to draw out of Londonderry for Belfast, I watched the big country girl on the platform being given farewell advice by her mother. The girl was obviously venturing to the big wicked city; she clutched a shiny suitcase in her clean-gloved hands, her hair was firmly battened down by a battalion of grips, her big country legs were encased in shiny stockings. 'Now never worry,' comforted her mother, 'everything will be all right. Ring me up the minute you get there, and don't be talking to no strange men. But never worry,' she repeated, 'for haven't I got the priest to give you a blessing, and I'll be saying the prayers for you, and then sure nothing can harm you.' She gave the girl a final pat on her haunches, and herded her into our compartment, where she sat in the opposite corner looking petrified. It was probably the first time she'd been away from home; certainly the first time she'd done so alone.

The sunny weather had turned quite chilly. I hugged my nice warm black cloak round me and wished there was some heating on the train. I stood up to get my book off the luggage rack, and kicked over the bulging plastic bag by my feet. Out rolled Baa Sinister, followed by the ornamental souvenir paperknife that Himself had bought in Port Na Blagh. There was a strangled gasp from the opposite corner as the poor girl took it all in – the black cape, the ram's horned skeletal head, the dagger . . .

She shrank back against the seat, appalled at being so soon assailed by the evils of the world, and spent the rest of the journey with her eyes closed, her lips moving in silent prayer, and her rosary flying through her fingers as she waited for me to draw a pentangle on the carriage floor. I just hoped the priest's blessing would prove strong enough to ward off the evil influence. Perhaps, along with all the other membership cards, we should now carry one from the Hellfire Club. You never know, it might even do nicely for booking flights. By broomstick, naturally.

Fran-tic Endeavours

I lay on the narrow piece of carpet between the beds, which was the only free space, and gazed speculatively at the ceiling. Was that a piece of hairy twine or an extra-heavy-duty cobweb hanging from the lampshade? It was amazing what a different perspective you got on things from a supine position. It was also quite comfortable, once you stopped doing exercises and breathing in fluff. The exercises were the real reason I was lying there, anyway; I wasn't supposed to be just reclining and noticing all the bits I hadn't cleaned. I'd better get on with a few movements, before I was overcome with guilt-feelings about my general slovenliness. (Unlikely, I admit, but just occasionally my conscience does give me a nudge, and I go into a whirlwind of domestic activity that has been known to last for as long as half an hour.) Some sit-ups would make a good start; they should do the trick, get rid of that embarrassing little pot belly which had developed lately, doubtless as a result of the wee buns and Pavlovas and Ulster fries . .

Five minutes later, having hacked my shin on the wardrobe and driven my stomach muscles into a frenzy of complaint, I lay back panting slightly and decided to call it a day. No point in ending up a physical wreck. Exercises would obviously take up too much effort and too much time. A diet, that was the answer. No more soda bread, no more wheaten farls, no more fruit scones, no more barmbrack – oh well, the sacrifice would be worth it, to get back the old sylphlike me. I hoped. Just cut down all round, that was best; I had no intention of embarking on any weird and wonderful diet that claimed to work miracles by restricting you to about three sorts of food, two of which were unobtainable outside Tibet and all of which were hugely expensive. Not after all that I'd been through with Fran. . . .

The moment I opened the office door the sound of crunching assailed me and I knew that the next few days were going to be sheer murder. Fran was on another of her diets. Fran's diets were notorious – she was addicted to them, and the fervour with which she plunged into each new one was matched only by the speed with which she abandoned it in favour of the next. If the promised miracle didn't happen within three days, she lost impetus; in the four months I'd been working with her, we had suffered together through the grapefruit diet, the banana, the hard-boiled egg, the bran-and-pineapple, the all-protein, the high-fibre, the high-fat, the low-fat and the herbal. None of them lasted more than a week and all, of course, had been completely ineffective.

Fran was a Big Girl, one of those whom Nature in her bounty and wisdom had designed on the grand scale. Rubens would have raved about her; the Victorians would have thought her A Fine Figure of a Woman. Unfortunately, she'd been born too late. This was the age of Twiggy, and the big girl was not in fashion. It wasn't that she was shapeless – far from it, she was all shape, with luscious sweeping curves from head to foot like a galleon under full sail. Unlike Venetia, who had been built like a Sherman tank, and was tall with it, Fran was medium height and swept in and out from bust to waist to hips like a magnificent roller-coaster. Her measurements were 42, 32, 44 and she longed for legs like matchsticks and a flat front, and vital statistics of 32, 23, 34.

Unfortunately, longing alone wasn't enough and she ate all the more to comfort herself. Dieting was her only hope of salvation, and heavens how she tried; but the overnight transformation she wanted never materialised. It was almost unbearable to watch her nibbling on the latest low-calorie lunch, and even worse to be surrounded by waste-paper baskets full of peel and eggshells. Worst of all, if I wanted to indulge in a sinful Mars bar or Crunchie, I had to go out into the loo and lock myself in, inspecting my teeth afterwards in the flyblown mirror to make sure there were no tell-tale traces left.

I wished desperately for Fran to meet a man who would love her for what she was, a beautiful full-blown paeony of a girl. But she was stuck on Shaun. Shaun, six foot two with a figure like a match with the wood scraped off. Shaun, who had piggy little eyes and legs like pipecleaners. Shaun, moreover, who never missed an opportunity to undermine her confidence by snide remarks about her weight, her shape and general lack of 'trendiness' – very important at the time. I hated Shaun, and he felt just the same about me. We sniped at each other constantly and this upset poor Fran all the more. She tried so hard to point out to each of us the other's good points, hard though they were to find, especially in his case. At least my nastiness was in Fran's defence.

As far as she was concerned, though, the sun shone out of the absurdly narrow seat of Shaun's flared jeans; *his* hips, of course, were minuscule. She thought him wonderful, possibly because he was the first man who had ever taken any notice of her. Even nasty notice was better than nothing.

Much against her principles, and much in advance of

the times, she had moved into his flat, which meant she got no respite from his gibes; it also meant that he had an unpaid skivvy and a cosy bed companion. No hot-water bottles or electric blankets were needed to warm Shaun's attenuated bones; I used to wonder if he wrapped her around him, like a billowing duvet. I also used to think, pleasurably, about what would happen if she rolled over on to him during the night; memories of sows overlaying their piglets stirred, and I lived in hope. Until that happy night, however, she was stuck with him as well as on him, and all I could do was try to bolster her confidence. I once suggested to Shaun, during a brief truce, that he might try this too, to which he replied that the only thing about Fran that reminded him of a bolster was her bosom. An unpleasant lad, as I said.

When she wasn't ingesting the latest miracle diet or slaving away for Shaun, Fran was a very hardworking and efficient secretary. The office was a kind of educational agency which dealt with a great many foreigners, and she sorted out their problems and language difficulties with tact, patience and understanding. I enjoyed the work too – one day we'd be surrounded by a gaggle of incredibly delicate little Oriental girls who made Fran feel huger than ever, and the next by whopping great culture-mad Scandinavians who made her feel comparatively fragile. Shaun dealt with bookings too. His attitude to foreigners was the ghastly one which insists that everyone born north of Watford or, even worse, over the Channel, is congenitally thick or deliberately obtuse. I wondered how he got away with the rudeness and contempt he displayed toward the clients until I cottoned on to the fact that he could switch in mid-sentence if the Boss came into the office. It was amazing – he could even change the tone of his voice halfway through a word, from the hectoring one he usually used to a sort of Uriah Heep obsequiousness that was almost worse.

But this particular morning Shaun was still out in the back office, drinking the tea that Fran had made for him and smoking her cigarettes because as usual he'd none of his own. (No doubt he'd grumbled at her for letting him run out.) For the moment, though, we had the front office to ourselves; just me, Fran and the crunching. 'This one's *bound* to work,' said Fran, looking up from her desk and speaking through a mouthful of what appeared to be raw celery judging by what I could see, which was quite a lot. Her face shone with a childlike faith. It was touching really, her eternal search for the secret, the diet which would overnight, or at least overweek, strip away the outer shell to reveal the slip of a girl concealed within. My heart sank. When I'd opened the office door and not been stunned by the pungency of oranges or the pervading pong of hard-boiled eggs, I'd hoped that for once we might start a working week without simultaneously starting a new regime for Fran. But she'd snuck up on me with this one, which turned out to be vast amounts of celery washed down with cups of weak black tea. It was a wonder her insides put up with it.

'You're guaranteed to lose at *least* ten pounds in a week,' Fran went on excitedly. I thought you might well lose a lot more, including the ability to stand upright, but from experience I knew better than to say anything; if she didn't lose three pounds overnight, she'd abandon the plan and go on to something even more outlandish. 'I've been on it since five o'clock last night,' she continued, 'and I'm *sure* I feel thinner already.' She rummaged in her desk drawer amongst the grubby powderpuffs and unsavoury hairbrushes until she found the tape measure. 'I'm going to take my measurements – my waist feels at least an inch smaller,' she announced hopefully, flinging the tape round and catching the end with the skill born of long practice. She measured herself at least once a day and it was never any different, but she kept on hoping. She was a born optimist; she had to be, living with Shaun.

She pulled the tape as tight as it would go without breaking, and tried to peer down to read it. Naturally, given the rolling acres of bosom in between, she couldn't see anything, so I had to bend down and squint. The tape was barely visible between the rolls of tummy, but even then the measurement remained a depressing 31½". Just to cheer her up, I told her it was 31, and she was thrilled. 'There,' she said, 'I *told* you it was working. Fancy, a whole inch off overnight!' I sat down at my desk and started work, wondering if I could stand three days of celery and weak tea. It wouldn't be easy, and I'd have to eat today's lunch – cold sausage and chutney sandwiches – well away from Fran's eyes. It would be cruel to sit there stuffing my face while she nibbled at yet another celery stalk.

A new intake of foreign students was due and we were frantically busy all morning, arranging accommodation, making bookings, all the usual carry-on. I hoped they'd turn out to be less trouble than the last lot; I was getting a bit tired of turning on the charm with department store managers in an effort to deflect shop-lifting charges. Some of the students seemed to regard Marks and Sparks as a positive challenge, a regular tourist attraction, and lifted whatever they could, whenever they could, whether they needed it or not. Sometimes I thought we ought to start issuing them with a sort of Nicking Certificate in recognition of their undoubted prowess; and the richer they were, the worse they were.

There was also the matter of the discreet arrangements which sometimes had to be made for certain little operations; some of the girls, free of strict parental control for the first time in their lives, went overboard with a vengeance and had to be rescued from the unfortunate, but inevitable, results of their folly. I always had to check whether or not they'd already had their appendix out. It would never have done to have informed Daddy that his precious daughter had had a second appendectomy.

But we had more serene hopes of this new lot, from North Africa; African students tended to be a lot less worrying, but did need quite a lot of tender loving care in order to settle them down. They found the damp English greyness depressing, they missed their extended families dreadfully, and they never seemed to have brought enough warm clothing; so the first step, usually, was to take them on a shopping spree for jerseys and vests and thick socks and boots, and then to entertain them at informal suppers and get-togethers until they'd found their feet and made a few friends of their own.

I just hoped that Shaun would keep out of the way when they arrived; he seemed to reserve his worst unpleasantnesses for black students, and his insolence made my toes curl with embarrassment. I knew Fran felt the same, and her lame, loyal attempts to make excuses for him were heart-rending. I just couldn't understand how she could go on trying to see a good side to the beastly man; but she stoutly maintained that he'd had an unhappy childhood, which had twisted him. I wasn't surprised; I could just imagine the sort of small boy he'd been, pulling wings off flies and pinching his schoolmates. She really was sorry for him, though; her soft heart pitied anyone who was so unpleasant, because to her way of thinking it must be because they were unhappy. It never occurred to her that he might be unhappy because he was so unpleasant.

'He *needs* me,' she would plead, when I was incensed about some extra-specially nasty remark he'd made to her. 'He needs to know I'll love him no matter *what* he does.' Privately I thought it would do him all the good in the world if she stood up to him and told him to get stuffed occasionally, but she'd been brought up in the pathetically mistaken belief that the love of a good woman could work miracles. It was sad, and I hated to see such an essentially loving woman being so exploited. It wasn't that she was blind to his faults, but somehow she had convinced herself that one day, if she just loved him and bore with him steadfastly enough, he would suffer a mighty sea-change and be magically transformed. Until then, she could only watch and pray, and I knew that secretly she was as glad as I was that he'd taken himself off on an unofficial message – down to the betting shop – when the expected group finally arrived.

There were six of them, four girls and two men – we were always overweighted with girls – and if they hadn't been so deep-frozen they'd have looked very colourful. As it was, their brilliant cotton robes and elaborate head-cloths framed faces grey and pinched by the November chill; their skins looked matt and dusty with cold, and I could see they were regretting this sudden transition to a seemingly inhospitable land. They'd come straight from the airport and they obviously needed warming up and cheering up, post-haste. Fran and I swung into our usual welcoming routine at once. She went out into the staff kitchen to rustle up tea and toast and instant soup, and I turned up the central heating so that it clanked and gurgled and at least it would sound as if it was trying to work up something approaching the equatorial heat to which they were accustomed. Then we sat them down and defrosted them before starting the necessary paperwork.

Once thawed out, they turned out to be a jolly, friendly lot; they were all planning to stay in London on various courses, ranging from secretarial through language to business studies, and a bit of culture-vulturing thrown in for good measure. One of the girls, Tandi, was enrolled in a sort of finishing-school course – English, flower-arranging, cordon bleu cookery, that sort of thing. She came from a diplomatic-corps family background, and had travelled a great deal. She was also very pleasant indeed, with a great sense of humour, and I looked forward to getting to know her better. She told us she had an older brother in England already, up at Oxford reading medicine; he was coming down at the weekend to make sure that she was settling in all right. Oh goody, I thought, another man – we were always desperately short of men for our regular Saturday evening 'getting-to-know-you' parties – so I leapt in and included him in the invitation. The party was usually held in one of the outer offices, which Fran and I laboured all Friday evening to transform into something a bit less bleak and more festive, with flowers and a few rather tatty paperchains left over from long-ago Christmases. We made the food, too, although sometimes, if we were lucky or hinted hard enough, one of the established students would bring along some of their home-made specialities, which were a lot more appetising than the thick-pastried sausage rolls and uninspired tinned stews which we managed to heat up in the ill-equipped kitchen.

This particular Saturday didn't look too promising. It was belting down with rain, I had a streaming cold and Fran was fraught. Shaun had grudgingly agreed to lend a hand and then skived off, probably to the bookies, taking the housekeeping money with him. Both he and the celery had let Fran down and she was fed up with the pair of them. The diet hadn't shifted another ounce and in addition had given her terrible wind.

No, she wasn't at her best, with no makeup and an unfortunate dress hauled in round the middle with a rope belt. It made her look, in my granny's succinct phrase, 'like a sack tied up ugly'. 'I don't *care*,' she sniffled miserably, stabbing the grilling sausages with unusual viciousness so that gouts of red-hot fat leapt and sizzled and flared up. 'I'm fat and plain and no one looks at me anyway.' 'Rubbish,' I told her callously, 'don't be so daft – that's Shaun talking, not you. You've got lovely hair, and gorgeous eyes, if you'd only slap a bit of eyeshadow on.' But she wouldn't, she just stood there, slumping, in a fine spray of sausage fat, feeling lumpy and unloved and thoroughly miserable. I'd never seen her so low, and I could see too that it wasn't the right moment for peptalks – we didn't have time, anyway, with the guests due any minute – so I gave her a quick hug in passing as I rushed out with a platter of sliced ham-and-egg pie. I arranged the food on the cloth as best I could to hide the stains, thumping the plates down and wishing I could thump Shaun instead. Perhaps Tandi, the nice African girl, could help; for all I knew, she could be related to a handy tribal medicine man, or even a witch doctor, who might be prevailed upon for assistance . . .

Just then the front door bell rang and put an end to my speculations.

The party was much like all the others; slow to start, with people standing about in stiff isolated clumps, trying to make conversation and wishing they'd stayed at home and read a book. English was obligatory, ostensibly to give everyone a common language, and naturally this made social chit-chat stilted. When Shaun attended he would sneer at the students' efforts in a very superior way. ' "Where you from?" ' he would mock, in the safety of the kitchen. ' "Are you many times in London?" "My father has much cattle." "In my country is much snow." Heavens above, you'd think they'd have something a bit more intelligent to say.' 'Oh Shaun, don't be so unkind,' Fran would plead. 'Perhaps they're just not used to this kind of party,' as if it were a glittering reception we were throwing instead of a cut-price student get-together. 'Yes, Shaun,' I put in, 'remember they haven't had all your social advantages, the poor ignorant souls. I mean, it's hard for someone like you to understand their difficulties, accustomed as you are to swapping epigrams in Mandarin with the international literati.' 'Shut up you,' responded the office Oscar Wilde, 'who's talking about oranges anyway?' I told him he gave me the pip and why didn't he just pith off. We made a great double act.

The party warmed up after a while, as they usually did once the horrible punch had circulated and the record player had exhausted its supply of polite background music and got around to the Rolling Stones. 'Hey You, Get Off Of My Cloud' and 'I Can't Get No Satisfaction' always worked wonders for everyone's camaraderie, if not for their English, no matter where they came from. Even Fran cheered up and fortified with a glass or so of cheap red wine, emerged from the kitchen to join us. A large German lad asked her to dance, and she circumnavigated the cleared centre of the room with him; he was very formal and correct and they looked rather majestic, marching round the floor amongst the gyrating bodies of the less inhibited.

I was bopping frenziedly with a small intense Mexican, with more hair on his chest than I had all over, when Tandi finally turned up. As promised, she had her brother in tow. I took one look, excused myself from Medallion Man and shot across to welcome them. It wasn't that the brother was terribly handsome or enormously tall or built like Mandingo. He wasn't. It wasn't even that he was strikingly robed. He was in jeans and a sweater. It was just that he wore the expression of a man who has been struck sharply and unexpectedly behind the ear with a sock full of wet sand. And he was looking straight at Fran.

His name, or at least his English name, was James. Tandi introduced us and I steered him over to the punch bowl and offered him a glass. He took a sip and blinked – it was that sort of punch – and came down to earth sufficiently to make small talk, in excellent English with a very elegant accent. But I could see that his mind wasn't really engaged. He managed to wrench his eyes away from Fran long enough to smile at me and be delightfully polite. After about two minutes he could obviously bear it no longer. 'Mrs W,' he said urgently, 'who, please, is that girl dancing with the tall fair man? Is she a student? Is that perhaps her boyfriend?' 'That's Fran,' I told him. 'She's not a student, she works here. And that's not her boyfriend,' I reassured him. No need to mention Shaun; he wasn't there, and if letting James think she was unattached meant a pleasant evening for Fran, so much the better. 'Would you like me to introduce you?' I offered. 'I would be most grateful, Mrs W,' he said, his eyes following Fran's stately progress around the room – the German had determination, to make up for his lack of a sense of rhythm. 'She is so beautiful, I would very much like to meet her. She is so natural, not all the makeup that the English girls like to put on, not the jeans. She is a *fine* woman – not thin, very strong, very healthy,' he added professionally. I remembered he was almost a doctor; he obviously had a gift for correct diagnosis.

Leaving him clutching his sticky glass of punch, I nipped across to rescue Fran. Fortunately the record came to an end and her partner was just bowing to her, practically clicking his heels, as I reached them. 'Say *danke schön* quickly, Fran,' I hissed, 'there's a gorgeous bloke over there who wants to be introduced. He's Tandi's brother and he's lovely, so be nice to him,' and I pushed her before me across to James before she could panic and seek sanctuary in the kitchen again. 'Fran, may I introduce James,' I gabbled. 'James, Fran is *very interested* in problems of nutrition,' and as the record player began to blast out 'Bubbling Brown Sugar', I seized the nearest man, a startled Japanese, and plunged back on to the floor. When I next caught sight of them, they were dancing like people possessed – Fran had discarded her restricting rope belt, her cheeks were flushed, her eyes sparkled, her beautiful hair flew round her head, all her generous curves were in glorious motion. She caught my eye. 'Oh, isn't this a lovely party!' she called, as she and James leapt and laughed. And by the end of the evening, they were in love.

Shaun was thoroughly unpleasant about the whole thing, of course, and for a while the situation was very nasty. Fran moved out of his flat and in with me the day after the party, and she had the courage to stay, despite Shaun's threats. She was racked with totally unnecessary guilt and pity, which he exploited to the full, but James was a constant source of confidence and comfort. He offered to talk it out with Shaun, man to man; but Shaun, typically, refused in terms which reduced Fran to still more tears, this time of disillusionment and anger that anyone could say such vicious things about the gentle, cultured James. Here was a man who loved her exactly as she was. Gone were the days of celery and black tea, of low-calorie drinks and cardboard slimming biscuits; she didn't need them any more; she had James. It was one of those sudden illogical mutual *coups de coeur* which can strike like lightning out of a clear sky, a sort of mutual instant recognition of one's other half. Any and all obstacles – and for James and Fran there were quite a few – only reinforce the bond, and eventually the obstacles are overcome. Fran left London, and so, after a year or so, did I, and that was the end of her story, or at least of my contact with her. But a couple of years ago, leafing through a *Tatler* in the dentist's waiting room, I came across a page of pictures taken at a diplomatic reception. There, smack in the centre, was a very clear photograph of James, and beside him, larger than ever and smiling blissfully, Fran, magnificent in flowing robes and high-swathed head-dress. The caption read, 'Mr O, the eminent surgeon, and his wife Francesca, who together have done so much to alleviate the suffering of the children of their country.'

I tore the page out, folded it carefully and put it into my handbag, and I didn't give a damn what the receptionist thought.

The Great House Search

It was a wild March day when the time definitely arrived to find a home of our own. Not that I had all that much against the flat; it was reasonably central, it had a fair amount of room, it was cheapish, and most important of all, Himself was deeply attached to the ramshackle place. But I felt an urgent need to find something more permanent, more private and, after the Ides of March incident, less open to the elements. Up until then, the flat might have been a bit shaky in parts but at least nothing had actually dropped off – which was a bit surprising really, considering its history. At the height of the Troubles, ages before I came on the scene, Himself had had a very rude awakening in the wee small hours one Sunday morning, being jolted out of a deep sleep to find himself on the floor with the long looking-glass and a major part of the ceiling lying on top of him. After a few befuddled moments during which he wondered what the hell he'd been drinking the night before that had caused him to wreck the joint, he was quite relieved to find it was only the result of a bomb which had gone off nearby. Gathering his wits and the shredded remnants of the bedspread round him, he picked his way down the rubble-strewn staircase to check on the elderly couple who were then living below. They were sitting up in bed, similarly plastered and bemused, and far from pleased at being so inconvenienced. The old lady, adjusting her curlers, clambered out of bed over the lumps of ceiling and headed for the kitchen. 'Tell me this and tell me no more,' she screeched at no one in particular, 'if they've gone and broke my teapot, I'll have their guts for garters so I will . . .'

The house had literally been shaken to its foundations, which explained the noisy stairs and why you had to shoulder-charge most of the doors to get them open. Once you'd got them shut in the first place. So I wasn't too surprised when, on the March day in question, the door to the rubbish room resisted all my efforts to get in there to excavate whatever it was I wanted. I flung myself against it several times, falling into the Christmas tree on the landing in my frenzy and sustaining a nasty wound to the tights. (The Christmas tree was still there in its bucket three months after Christmas because it was trying so hard to stay green, and I hadn't the heart to throw it out; besides, it came in handy for hanging stuff on, like washed knickers and notes to Himself saying things like what kind of a time is this to come home, your dinner's in next-door's dog.)

I wished I knew how policemen opened doors in films, kicking them neatly and effectively just under the handle, but with my athletic prowess I was likely to end up with a fractured tibia and a still firmly closed door. Slow, steady, unremitting pressure – the tortoise method rather than the hare – would surely work in the end. So I turned the knob until the little metal bit that fits into the door jamb was free of its slot, and pushed the door the tiny bit it *would* go, to stop the latch catching again. Then I lay down on the landing on my back, put my feet against the panels and, hanging on to the least wobbly banisters for purchase, pushed as hard as I could. It was a bit like having a baby only lower down, and just as productive. After several minutes' hard work, during which I turned a fetching shade of puce and the banisters bent like longbows, the door began to inch inwards. Soon I could put my head into the room to see what was jamming it; I expected to see that the dozen assorted anoraks, sailing jackets and ancient overcoats had fallen off their hooks on the back of the door. But instead, oh horrors, a great pile of plaster, brick, torn wallpaper and thick black dirt lay all over the room, and opposite me stood nothing but bare laths and the back of next-door's bedroom wall. The whole wall had been stripped off and, now that the door was open the wind howled in, stirring up the dust of ages. Looking up in stunned dismay I saw that the skylight, glass and frame and all, had disappeared . . .

Himself got hold of the landlord, the landlord got hold of the builder, and I got hold of a large whisky with no water. The builder said the wind had sucked out the skylight, the resulting vacuum had sucked down the wall, and he might be able to come and see to it in a couple of weeks. In the meantime, the best he could do was a tarpaulin over the gaping hole in the roof.

I was horrified; apart from the muck and masonry lying all over some of my most treasured possessions, like my offspring's childhood fingerpaintings and the certificate saying I had mastered the kiss of life, I dreaded the thought that with the wall open to the rafters, we were quite open to visitations from all sorts of unwelcome visitors. Mice, spiders, maybe even bats – but worse, the way was now clear for the Rat's Revenge; goodness knows what we might expect . . . They had waited a long time.

The Episode of the Rat had begun shortly after the walls were first breached by the bomb. Himself, living happily alone in the bachelor informality which means food left lying on the table for days on end, became puzzled by mysterious inroads in the butter and teeth marks on the cheese. Also, a freshly opened packet of bacon, left handily on the draining board, disappeared, leaving the wrapper in the middle of the floor. Himself blamed it on the resident mice and merely set a small trap. It caught nothing. A discarded sock disappeared next, from the bedroom floor, but this was no great surprise to a man who could rarely find a matching pair anyway and its significance was overlooked. It wasn't until a handkerchief vanished overnight from the bedside table that he got really worried. If these were mice, they were big, strong, extra sneaky mice. One morning the breadknife handle was found to be chewed out of all recognition. And then, returning from the club one night, Himself reached the top of the stairs to be confronted by the culprit – King Rat himself, with bristling whiskers and snake-like tail, and apparently the size of your average dachshund. Even allowing for Irish exaggeration, he must have been a nasty sight, especially as he stood his ground for several long seconds before scurrying off. Himself swears the creature growled at him.

Obviously the situation called for something more drastic than an ordinary mousetrap. Himself was in favour of a sawn-off shotgun at the very least, but after taking advice from his friendly local Rodent Operative, who reckoned that the Beast of Belfast had been routed from his usual sewery haunts by the explosion, a sticky compound was applied to the kitchen floor and Himself went off to work with high hopes of success. He hadn't, unfortunately, given any thought at all to what the next step would be should the super-glue do its job.

When he came home, he could hear the shrill screeching as soon as he opened the front door, and he hit the stairs running. The noise was bloodcurdling; and there in the kitchen was the frantic rat, held horribly to the adhesive by its hind legs. Himself was appalled. There was only one thing to do and he very bravely did it. He seized his heavy blackthorn stick and dealt the coup de grâce, as swiftly and mercifully as he could. After which he went straight across the road to the nearest pub and had three unaccustomed doubles, rather quickly. It was the way the rat looked him straight in the eyes just before he hit it, he said. He felt like a murderer.

So now I was convinced that all the King Rat's relatives, thirsting for blood, would be planning revenge for the regicide. I pictured them massing in the rafters, muttering and plotting and deciding which of us to eat first. Any untoward nocturnal sound, even some toward ones, was enough to fetch me upright in bed, eyes straining into the blackness, ears flapping for the ominous patter of a thousand ratty feet. We didn't see a sign of anything, of course, but that was only because they were so cunning and wanted to lull us into a sense of false security. It was only a matter of time before horror-stricken neighbours would find us in our beds, two middle-aged skeletons stripped clean by the Midnight Avengers . . .

I bought the local newspaper, visited all the house

agents, and began the search for sanctuary immediately. I was sick of sitting up all night with a tennis racket in my hand.

I am convinced that all estate agents are descended in an unbroken line from the mediaeval troubadours – those outwardly romantic but inwardly pragmatic souls who wandered across the realm from one castle to the next, earning their living by composing and singing endless ballads of undying love and admiration. Outwardly romantic; but let no one be deceived. Ballads were their daily bread, poetry their stock in trade, hyperbole their crafty craft. Faced with a princess who, on a good day with the light behind her, resembled the back of a stout rampart, did they sing of her dull frontal aspect and large, rambling rear elevation? Did they heck. They sang of her charming period features and unlimited potential. Any lady unlucky enough to be wall-eyed would be serenaded on her incomparable panoramic outlook, while her sister with the unfortunate weakness for day-glo wimples would be lauded to the skies for her tastefully imaginative décor.

Only centuries of poetic licence, of discriminatory double-think, could have resulted in the average house agent's ability to turn a pretty phrase and a selective blind eye. Over the next few months I became an authority on their flights of fancy.

The trouble is, I fall for it every time. Goodness knows why; it's not that I'm gullible in any other area. Politicians' promises elicit only a cynical 'Oh yeah?' and soap powder commercials leave me cold. Nor do cosmetic manu-facturers' claims send me rushing out hot-foot to buy the latest miracle cream. But houses . . . Years of trying to be a pessimist – because then you only get *pleasant* surprises – haven't been entirely successful; somewhere deep down is a yearning romanticism which doggedly surfaces from time to time. Couple this with my lifelong love affair with the written word – as a child I thought that reading was what your life was *for*, and read every-thing within reach, including sauce bottles (*'Cette sauce de haute qualité'*) and San Izal toilet paper – and you can see what an easy mark I am for estate agents. A real sucker. I honestly believe every word. I *want* 'character-ful' to mean beams and inglenooks rather than poky rooms and a kitchen where you can't see to speak the truth; when they say 'conservatory' I visualise a Victorian gem of curved glass and banked ferns, not a 3 foot by 4 foot plastic extension containing two dead cyclamens and the dog's bowl.

Never mind that reality has never once come up to my imaginings. To be truthful, it never could; but hope goes on springing eternal that *one* day, somehow, somewhere, I shall find, for a mere song, my perfect dream house. With modern plumbing, Victorian conservatory, beams, inglenook fireplace, spiral staircase, tower bedroom, widow's walk, stone walls, pantry, walk-in wardrobes, farmhouse kitchen, sloping ceilings, built-in cupboards, panelled study . . . And oh boy, will it be *characterful*.

Meanwhile, however, I got to grips with the balladeers of Belfast. Every lunchtime I hurtled out of the office, aflame with naïve enthusiasm, to view yet another prospect, only to trail back, disillusioned. But the disillusion never lasted; the next day I'd go off again, certain that this would be *it*. One house description particularly took my fancy: compact pied-à-terre, it said, convenient for town, easy upkeep, low outgoings, perfect for young couple. I disregarded the young bit – after all, we were fairly *new*, which was almost the same – and set off full of optimism. When I finally found the place, it turned out to be miles from anywhere; obviously only convenient for car owners. Compact it certainly was. There was a minute sitting room, about six foot square; a kitchen which I mistook for a cupboard; one bedroom full of bed; and a bathroom where you could sit on the loo and wash your hair in the basin at the same time. Actually you could *only* use the basin if you sat on the loo. The low outgoings proved to be the doors; I had to stoop to get in and Himself would very likely have had to enter on hands and knees. Pied-à-terre obviously meant exactly what it said. You could put only one foot on the floor at a time, anywhere. In a despairing effort to create the illusion of more space, a former tenant (possibly a midget) had stuck mirror tiles all over the sitting-room walls. The effect was terrifying. But the house did, it really *did*, have character, even if the promised potential was that of making you feel like Alice after she accepted the invitation on the bottle labelled 'Drink Me'. And it was cheap. For a fleeting few minutes I flirted with the idea of turning it into a hideaway just for me. It was tempting; I could have my own establishment, live on take-aways from the Chinese round the corner and, when I felt lonely, invite Himself over for a bit of social chit-chat and a quick Spring Roll. Who knows, if the mood took us, even the mirror tiles might come into their own . . . But the notion died a quick death. I couldn't possibly forfeit those gorgeous Ulster fries of a morning.

The next place I sallied forth to inspect sounded more likely. Over the phone, the agent assured me that the rooms were of good size, there was a modern bathroom and a garage, and although the house needed a little work done on it this was, in the phrase beloved of his ilk, 'reflected in the asking price'. 'It's a charming property,' he added. The thought of a garage definitely appealed; we had no car but we did have an awful lot of junk. I arranged to meet the man at lunchtime.

It was a terraced house, badly in need of paint, but I took this to be the necessary 'little work'. The charm, though, wasn't immediately apparent even to my credulous eye. Perhaps I would step straight into it when we got inside. The agent, beaming, opened the front gate. It came off in his hand. 'Just needs a couple of new hinges,' he said brightly, leaning the gate up against the hedge and inserting the key in the front door. He pushed it open and ushered me in ahead of him.

What I stepped into wasn't charm, but a fairly large hole. I shot down about nine inches, landing on a mixture of rubble, junk mail and several ancient Kentucky Fried Chicken containers complete with bones. Aghast, the agent extricated me, apologising wildly. I think he thought I might sue. 'I can't understand it,' he kept saying plaintively. 'It must have happened since I was last here.' I wondered just how long the place had been standing empty; some of the junk mail I recognised as stuff we'd had inflicted on us months ago. The poor man was in such a state that I felt sorry for him; I determined to find the rest of the house delightful, just to make him feel better.

It wasn't easy. It was impossible. Try as I might, the words of appreciation died in my throat. I didn't know which of us was the more embarrassed as we picked our way from room to room, reading the description and then facing the reality. 'This,' he announced bravely, 'is the modern kitchen.' 'I see,' I said, gazing at the stone sink, the holey lino, the splintery work surfaces covered in stick-on plastic. We went upstairs, carefully avoiding a missing tread. 'The bathroom,' he cried, flinging open the door, 'with coloured suite,' and choked a little as the room was revealed. Over the bath there was a hole in the ceiling. And in the roof. The bath itself, the side panel peeling away, was half-full of rain water, black with soot and no doubt seething with amoebae and possibly frogs. The lavatory seat, in two halves, lay on the floor. Whoever had used the loo last had neglected to flush it. The washbasin was cracked. I could hardly bear to look at the agent's face. He was only a young man, and it wasn't his fault. My heart went out to him. 'Perhaps we could go and see the garage?' I suggested gently.

I shouldn't have. It didn't do any good. The garage turned out to be a shed of sorts, but the most obvious thing about it was that it was totally inaccessible. The terraced houses were built back to back, rear garden adjoining rear garden, and there was no alleyway between. I was sorry to have to cause him more pain, but it was puzzling. 'How on earth would you get a car *in* here?' I enquired. Beaten, he surveyed the shed, the surrounding walls, the totally enclosed patch of ground. He turned his eyes to me, pleadingly. 'Helicopter?' he suggested brokenly.

* * *

So it went on. Either alone or with Himself I spent months at it. There was the flat painted throughout in bright salmon pink – doubtless a job lot of bargain-priced paint, unless the owner's mother had overdosed on John West's during pregnancy. There was the cottage with floorboards like lace, from woodworm. There was the house belonging to a friend, which turned out on survey to have a monstrous growth of dry rot under the bedroom floor. The flat where you had to pass four other front doors to reach the bathroom. The attic studio where a former tenant had, I discovered by accident, burned to death, beating her fists against the unopenable windows. The dear little house that we loved and lost, pipped at the post by a buyer with cash in hand – that took a lot of getting over. The damp ones, the dirty and dreary and derelict ones, the overpriced, the undermined, the ones that needed thousands spent on them. Even my eternal optimism was faltering under the strain.

One Sunday, armed with the usual fistful of romantic fiction, we set out on a fairly low-key expedition. We'd pored over the street map and worked out our itinerary; first, the terraced cottage in the Holy Land, an area comprising streets with such names as Jerusalem, Palestine and Carmel. Then, over the river to the avenues bearing names echoing past glories of Empire – Kandahar, Delhi and Karachi. Then, if our strength held out, up to the more prosaic North Parade and Ravenhill Road. We didn't really expect to find anything. But as it turned out, we got no further than the Holy Land.

It didn't look like much from the outside. Very narrow, a door and window on the ground floor and two windows above; a minute strip of front garden. The owners were in, a charming young couple now moving from this, their first home, to another in the suburbs where they'd have a garden for the expected baby. We went in, we looked round. There was much more to it than could be guessed from the frontage. Admittedly the sitting room was small, and there were no beams or inglenooks, but there was a brand-new kitchen and bathroom – with a coloured suite. There were two bedrooms, and an attic which, while not in a tower, definitely had *potential*. Most

important of all, the house felt friendly. It liked us, and we liked it. We sat and chatted, we had tea and sandwiches, we left to view the properties across the river.

Three silent minutes away from the house, we stopped. I looked at Himself and he looked back at me. 'That's the one I want,' I said. 'So do I,' said Himself, and as one we turned and pelted back the way we'd come. In the short time since we'd left, the owners had gone out. I was distraught. Frenziedly, I scrabbled through my pockets and unearthed an old shopping list. Fortunately Himself had a pen, and I crossed out 'Lge loaf cot. cheese pol.vod.' and wrote, 'We'll take it! Don't sell it to anyone else, please!', signed our names and shoved it through the letter box. And then we went home and waited.

The gods must have been on our side, because we got it. The building society man was a perfect lamb; obviously, beneath the dark business suit beat a heart filled with pure romance. He listened to my impassioned tale of love at first sight and, clearly moved, agreed to accept the major part of our earnings for the rest of our lives. After that, all that remained to be done was to vacate the flat. Goodbye to the cracks in the walls, the knickers in the yard, the dark mysterious stain on the floorboards where the rat made his Last Stand. Farewell to our first shared home. I think Himself found it more of a wrench than he'd expected; a lot had happened to him while he'd been living there. Including me.

Even I felt a pang as we manhandled the last load of belongings down the creaking stairs. I wondered if the next tenants would paint the patchy bathroom walls and obliterate the heart saying 'I love I.W.' that I drew with lipstick on my first night there. I bet they did. Some people have no souls.

On Probation

'Here I am again girls, beautiful as ever!' trilled the apparition in the doorway. Evelyn, Maggie and I, three handmaidens of the probation service, raised our eyes from our work and surveyed the visitor. We blinked involuntarily as the full impact of the vision of sheer, if startling, delight hit home. Fuchsia platform clogs, skin-tight cerise satin jeans and a rainbow-hued Lurex blouse are a bit too much to take early on a Monday morning, particularly when topped, as these were, by diamanté sunglasses and a tumble of shoulder-length daffodil curls. As one, we sighed resignedly. 'Come on in, Charlie,' groaned Evelyn. 'What the hell is it this time?'

Having made the desired impression, Charlie lowered the cerise stretchies cautiously into the nearest chair and beamed at us. We failed to beam back. Charlie's visits usually meant one thing only – trouble for him and work and worry for us. 'Any charnst of a cuppa then, ducky?' he enquired. He removed the Farrah Fawcett-type wig and heaved a sigh of relief. 'Cor, them things is murder,' he added. 'Dunnarf make yer 'ead sweat.' He flung the wig on to my desk, where it lay like a collapsed haystack while he enjoyed a lengthy therapeutic scratch of his few remaining wisps of natural hair. He had his teeth in today; it made a nice change. I put the kettle on. It was far too early for elevenses, but there was no point in telling

Charlie that; there'd be no peace until he got his cuppa, with plenty of milk and three sugars. He had a sweet gum, did Charlie.

Evelyn returned to the attack. 'Well, what is it?' she asked. 'What've you done now?' Charlie put on his aggrieved-innocence face, which he was good at because he used it a lot. 'You innarf 'ard-'earted, Ev,' he complained. ''Ow jer know I ain't just come for a chat with me friends?' 'Because I know you, Charlie, and so does Maggie, and so does Ann. So don't try the old flannel on us,' she warned, 'because it won't work.'

The trouble was, it always did. Charlie was one of our longest-established clients; he was one of life's born losers and he did blow-all to slow down the process, let alone reverse it. Heaven only knows what his background was. Even our comprehensive files, of which Charlie's was about six inches thick, had failed to plumb it. But it must have been extraordinary; certainly his foreground was spectacular enough. He had absolutely nothing going for him. He was a petty thief, he was unemployable, completely untrustworthy and as bent as a corkscrew. The poor probation team had spent years of their thankless lives trying to help him; but he was practically unhelpable. Over and over again, a job would be found for him; not a demanding job, just some sort of paid work. Sometimes, if they were lucky, he'd stay in it for as much as a week, but not often. One winter he came in complaining bitterly of the cold; they found him a nice warm job sweeping up in a doctor's surgery. Within three days he'd downed broom and scarpered, together with a wad of prescription forms. 'Wouldn't let me wear me wig,' was all he offered by way of explanation when they caught up with him.

He got into fights with his boyfriends and then turned up at our office with bruises and black eyes, sobbing his fishnet socks off and begging us to set the coppers on that big butch bully what done it. He was awful, I suppose; but despite everything he had a certain charm, a cheeringly brave refusal to be beaten down by the sordid circumstances of his life. One minute there he'd be, snivelling his way through my box of tissues and whining that the bloody social security didn't care if he lived or died – hardly surprising, he pestered them even more than he pestered us – and the next he'd perk up, remark that it didn't do no good looking on the black side, and what did we think of this new shade of eyeshadow what he'd lifted from Woolies? The word 'incorrigible' could have been coined just for him.

Today, however, he was in good form; for once, he really had just come for a chat. He drank his tea and sucked one of Maggie's custard creams. His teeth didn't fit very well, because they'd been made for someone else originally, and sometimes he took them out to tackle a biscuit. It was better when he settled for sucking. We got on with our typing, to discourage conversation and to cover the noise, but it wasn't very effective. He put down his cup. 'Ta,' he said. 'Wodjer think of the blouse, then?' He smoothed it, preening, over his painfully narrow chest. We thought for a moment. The truth would never do. 'Very gay,' remarked Maggie, hitting the nail smartly on the head. She had a flair for the right word. 'Just what I thought,' Charlie said happily, 'soon's I saw it, I thought, that's very gay, that is. So I pulled it out straight away, as the bishop said to the actress.' 'Out of *what*?' we chorused, ignoring the last bit: Charlie spent half his time trying to shock us. 'The dustbin, o' course, ducky,' he said, 'be'ind them flats up the road. I didn't steal it, honest— look 'ere, there's stains on it, there was potato peelin's on it when I found it.' The prospect of a closer inspection wasn't enticing. 'We'll believe you, Charlie,' I said, 'thousands wouldn't.' Charlie bridled. He decided, having got outside his tea and biscuits, to take umbrage. ' 'Ere I am,' he complained woundedly, 'tryin' to be honest, tellin' you the truth, and what good does it do me?' He replaced the haystack, with some dignity. ' 'Ow can I be expected to go straight? Nobody *trusts* me, that's the trouble.' And, tossing his flamboyant head, he flounced out. A triple valediction of 'Too right,' 'Ain't it the truth' and 'You've guessed it, Charlie' floated after him.

Charlie was really one of the least of our worries. The only problem with him was warding off the gifts he frequently pressed upon us; sachets of shampoo from the next-door chemist, scarves and hankies from local department stores. All nicked, out of the kindness of his heart and in the hope that we wouldn't realise it. It was very difficult. If we accepted them we became receivers of stolen goods, and if we reported him, with his record it would probably have meant a spell inside; and he was terribly prone to get raped in prison, which he didn't relish any more than anyone else. His love-life may have been bizarre to some – he once telephoned in a panic to say that he was bleeding to death from a vicious bite inflicted by a jealous lover; decency forbids me to specify where it was, but applying a tourniquet could have been very tricky – but he had his standards. He liked to choose his partners. But he never frightened us, even when he threw a tantrum; he was more like a petulant, unpredictable child. Paddy, now, was something else altogether . . .

If I'd been able to see into the future, I might well have had second thoughts about throwing in my lot with

Himself – because Paddy was a wild Irishman, and I mean *wild*. He scared the living daylights out of me, and the probation officer unfortunate enough to have him as a client had my awed admiration. She was a tiny, bird-boned girl; he was six foot two and as wide as a barn door. She was in her twenties; he was sixty-odd. Her background was middle-class, private school, university. His family had been itinerant tinkers and he could neither read nor write. But he could shout and he could swear, and most of the time he did both at once. Every time he came to see her I was convinced he would kill her, but she just took him into her office and shut the door. I hovered anxiously in the corridor, listening to his roars and her refined little interjections. I was terrified he would attack her with his stick – he had a great blackthorn that he used to brandish at startled passers-by in the street, and once he had burst into our office and demolished Evelyn's waste-paper basket with it.

The probation officer must have had the right touch, though; the roars would die down to a dull rumble, and eventually she would open her door and, none the worse for the harrowing half-hour, usher him out. Paddy didn't actually commit any very serious crimes; he was had up regularly for drunk-and-disorderly, or threatening behaviour, which meant that he had taken amiss the public's failure to appreciate his rendition of Irish ballads outside the Co-op. Once he had drink taken, which was roughly whenever he wasn't asleep, he got fiercely homesick for the Auld Sod, and would periodically importune the authorities until, in desperation, they repatriated him. He would be away for a blissful couple of months, but then the siren call of the Kilburn High Road would entice him again, we would hear the familiar bellowing rising from the streets below, and Maggie, looking out of the window, would announce, 'I see the Auld Sod's back in business.' It was like the swallows returning.

Apart from Paddy's assault on the waste-paper bin, we didn't have much actual violence to cope with. But we did have to get used to verbal abuse and it was hard not to get cynical as a result. Some of the clients regarded us as the greatest fools going, and didn't hesitate to let us know it; they lumped all the government agencies together as the enemy, to be despised and duped. As with Charlie, a job would be found for someone, often with great difficulty. The client would turn up for a day or so, and then pack it in. '*Why?*' we would plead. 'Why did you give it up? It was a *job*, you had a *wage* – what happened?' 'Meant getting up at eight in the morning, dinnit? Couldn't be bothered.' Little wisps of steam would begin to issue from Evelyn's ears. 'Good thing for you we don't feel like that,' she'd explode – she had an artistic temperament and a powerful inborn Protestant work-ethic. 'Here we are at the crack of dawn [a slight exaggeration] working our fingers to the bone [another, larger one] on your behalf!' 'More fool you then – catch me gettin' outa bed before the streets are aired . . .' It was a whole new philosophy. I stopped feeling guilty about lying in until ten o'clock on a Sunday.

Rita definitely didn't want a job. She had an occupation already: she was a full-time complete mess. Unlike Charlie, who was a mess too but had redeeming qualities, Rita had no saving graces whatsoever as far as I could see. She was such a *wet* – self-pity oozed out of her like water out of a sodden sock. It was hard to summon up compassion for someone so convinced that the world not only owed her a living but should somehow contrive to do the tiresome business of living for her. She was passivity incarnate. Things just happened to her – how or why she had no idea, and she had no interest in finding out. Babies kept arriving – she had five, and she was twenty-three – but the pill was too difficult to remember about and she didn't fancy the coil and by the time the idea of anything else surfaced, it was usually too late anyway. The family debts were astronomical, and the hire purchase people ran a regular service, taking away the furniture or the telly.

She would come into the office and sit there, bedraggled and bemused, and recount the latest blow that an unfeeling fate had dealt her. 'The kids keep gettin' colds,' it might be. 'Someone'll 'ave to do somethin', I can't cope with it all, what can *I* do?' We would suggest, gently, that perhaps a woolly jumper might be more suitable, in this weather, than an outgrown T-shirt. 'There ain't none left – they're all dirty,' she would sigh plaintively. 'Someone'll 'ave to give me some more . . .' Could she, perhaps, wash one or two, just to keep things going? 'I can't – I tried once and they went all matted . . .' Next time, 'It's the gas people,' she'd moan, absently slapping at one of her brood. 'Samantha, leave the lady's skirt alone, she don't want your lolly all over it. Oh dear, sorry love, I can't do nothin' with 'er. It's the gas, like I said. I told 'em, I can't pay, 'oos gonna pay? My ol' man, Reet, he said, what you done with the 'ousekeeping, but I dunno, I can't seem to manage . . .' And on and on she'd go. If it wasn't the gas it was the electric, or the rent, or the catalogue payments, or the tallyman. And somehow, simply by folding up and abdicating all responsibility, she succeeded in getting someone else to pay, or cope, or supply clean sweaters. Every time. Perhaps she wasn't so stupid after all. I went along on a visit to her flat once; it was a tip, but all four bars of the sitting-room fire were on, the oven was on with the door open 'to warm the kitchen up', and there were fan heaters going full blast in all three bedrooms. It was like a hot-house – no wonder the kids got colds.

I went home to my own economically chilly flat in an even more disillusioned frame of mind than usual, and I admit it – I put on two panels of the gas heater instead of only one. What the hell, I thought. More fool me, for reading in bed night after night with my gloves on.

In our probation office, we didn't have any real villains to deal with. Mostly the clients were like Charlie and Rita – misfits, inadequate flotsam on the sea of life. There was no real bad in them, no viciousness. They just couldn't cope without endless support, and never would be able to. They floated on from day to day, from crest to trough, managing somehow to keep their heads above water but with no chance of making it to the shore. In a different age, a less urban, less sophisticated, less technological world, they might have been better off; they might have pottered through life well enough in an undemanding sort of way. As it was, everything was a bit too much for them. They were largely illiterate (although Charlie enjoyed magazines, and lifted *Harper's Bazaar* and *Queen* regularly), having left school at the first opportunity after being written off by their teachers at the age of seven. Sport was something to be watched, or a tribal allegiance and a good excuse for a punch-up. Telly-watching, or going down the pub, were their main hobbies. Plus, of course, the pools – though how they would have coped with the problems engendered by a big win made the mind boggle.

Not that they were despondent or downhearted; far from it. Most of them were extraordinarily cheerful and relatively buoyant. There was, for instance, Bella – she certainly had a high old time. She was big and black and very beautiful, and she never said no to anything, which was what had landed us with her. Equally, she never regretted anything either, so that it was hard for her to appear appropriately repentant when she was hauled up yet again for doing something which had seemed like a good idea at the time. It went on seeming like a good idea to Bella, an attitude that led her into trouble with alarming regularity. She enjoyed everything and everybody with great gusto and complete impartiality; a little drink, a bit of a whingding, a spot of breaking and entering, some lighthearted shoplifting, they were all part of life's rich tapestry to her, and one was no worse than another. If 'incorrigible' was Charlie's word, 'amoral' was Bella's.

And 'piteous' was the one to describe Peter. Once a man quite well-up in his profession, he had been the son of a domineering woman who had frightened off any girl who came anywhere near him. His father, having once made the necessary biological contribution, had been discarded – Peter never knew him except through his mother's lurid disparagements. Men in general, he was brought up to believe, were dirty, brutish, and obsessed with sex; women, on the other hand, were almost without exception pure, virtuous and highminded. The exceptions being any girls who showed any interest whatsoever in Peter. They, naturally, were scheming trollops from whom he must be protected for his own good. As a result, by the time Peter was a young adult he had decided it was safer, in the face of the appalling threat implicit in adult sexuality, to have nothing at all to do with it. Decent women were not for besmirching, and men of course were out of the question, even as friends. Better to stay at home with mother, who loved you in spite of your being a male, and who, if you were a very good boy, might even forgive you for it.

So he stayed with mother, in the permanent role of obedient son, constant companion and lackey, until she died. He was fifty and he didn't have a friend in the world. Depression hit him like a ton of lead, and within months he had lost his job, sold his mother's house to make ends meet, and moved into a cheap and nasty flat. There, claustrophobically hemmed in with the heavy old-fashioned furniture from home, he sat alone and stared at the wall for days on end, and thought about ending such an empty and lonely existence. Later, perhaps he wished he'd had enough courage; if he'd known what was coming, he would have summoned it up from somewhere.

The really tragic part of his life began with something which, in other circumstances, could have been a blessing; the local children began calling at his door. Unfortunately, they didn't call with any idea of doing good deeds or cheering up the new tenant who they had noticed lived alone; they came, mainly, to see what they could get from him. And he, grateful for any company, gave them money for sweets and the pictures. After a while they made it plain that their visits were conditional on the money; no cash, no company. He paid up. Then one or two of the children, more street-wise and mercenary than the others, decided to take matters a step or two further. They traded on his longing for affection, tempted him into actions which, although nowhere near as wicked as they might have been, were still wrong. He tried to resist, he told them to go away, so they said they would tell their parents that he'd done it anyway. So poor, weak, mixed-up Peter was caught in the trap. He paid up and paid up, in return for the forbidden favours which he would be charged with anyway. And in the end, of course, he got caught; as of course he had to be, and needed to be: but it finished him altogether. He was given a gaol sentence, from which he emerged psychologically and physically beaten. The authorities had their eye on him, naturally, and by the time the probation service tried to help him he was a wreck. Even the watchful police were sorry for him – they knew the children involved – but the law is the law, and rightly so. Not long after I came to know him, he was arrested again, on suspicion of importuning a minor. They put him into the cells, and when they went to rouse him in the morning he was dead. 'I couldn't stand another stretch inside – I'd sooner die,' he had wept to Maggie and me, only two weeks before. There certainly wasn't much left for him to live for, and I was glad that it was all over.

Working in the probation service was never dull and frequently rather more exciting than one had bargained for. All human life was certainly there, and it proved that there was more in heaven and earth than was dreamed of in *my* philosophy anyway. I loved it, even though it drained the emotions; even as a humble secretary I found myself lying awake at night worrying over clients like Peter or even, occasionally, Charlie. It was such a contrast from my previous job, working as a housekeeper for the wealthy and privileged, but it had one thing in common with that – it showed me a side of life that I had never realised existed. As a cook housekeeper, I saw a section of society which lived in a style vastly different from my own – moneyed, leisurely, often frivolously idle. In the probation service I saw the other side; equally idle sometimes, but more often desperately deprived. It was an eye-opening experience and sometimes a heartbreaking one.

I spent two action-packed and happy years with Evelyn and Maggie, and might well have stayed until I qualified for the obligatory retirement clock in recognition of time served. It was around this time, however, that Himself made his fateful entrance into my life; and after a while we decided that time spent living apart was time wasted. As any thought of his leaving Ulster threw him into severe culture shock, it was up to me to uproot myself. I gave in my notice, rather sadly, and we swung into the old familiar round of farewells. Charlie nicked me a super going-away present and told me not to do anything he wouldn't do. I promised him I wouldn't.

Make Do and Mend

Charlie's problem was, of course, that he was beset by sudden urges which he was totally unable – not to mention unwilling – to resist. So was Bella, and so were most of the other clients of the probation office. They are not alone. On Sundays, for instance, I get this irresistible impulse to strip. Even though I know from dire experience how it will turn out, the temptation is overpowering. This time, I think, this time I'll be strong-willed; this time I'll stop before I go too far. I won't get carried away; I'll be discreet; if I hide here behind the dining-room door and just rip off this one little . . .

And the next thing you know, there it is, naked. A great bare patch of wall. And there am I, with a four-inch-wide, five-foot-long piece of wallpaper in my hand. Blood lust has won, and I go into a positive frenzy of vandalism, regardless of the consequences. It's so *satisfying*. There's nothing to match the glow of achievement when you manage to detach a whole panel, from floor to ceiling, in one glorious sweep . . . Within minutes the room is knee-deep in paper and Himself is aghast. He has seen what the wallpaper has been mercifully concealing, and knows what he is in for. And when we moved into Workman's Warren, he was in for plenty.

When the house was finally ours, we transferred ourselves and all our clobber with great enthusiasm and

116

the help of assorted kind friends and their transport. One or two of them, cars and friends, winced a bit when they saw the mountain of stuff we wanted to cram into their boots and on to their roofs, but at last it was all unloaded and dumped. We spent the next week or so humping furniture about, developing muscles like Charles Atlas and discovering that wardrobes and narrow stairs don't mix. I kept reminding Himself, in tones of infuriatingly sweet reason, that the previous owners had removed their bedroom suite *somehow*, and that what goes down must go up, until it was all he could do not to drop a bedstead on me. It was months before we discovered that they'd had to remove the bedroom windows and get it out with a block and tackle.

Finally everything was pretty much where we wanted it, or at least in the only place where it would fit. Having the desk in the bathroom may be unusual, but it's jolly handy for those moments when inspiration strikes when you're on the loo, as it so often does.

After we'd got the place into some sort of order, we relaxed for a bit and got our breaths back, and that was when I fell into temptation in the dining room. That woodchippy sort of paper is the most enticing in the world, and it was but the work of a moment to slip a fingernail under a badly glued edge in an exploratory sort of way. Once I heard the first crisp crackle there was no holding me; I could no more stop tearing than stop breathing. It was bliss. Himself was transfixed in front of the telly in the sitting room – France were playing Ireland – and I really let myself go. Yards of paper were wreathed around my ankles, the air was filled with flying plaster where I had gouged too enthusiastically with the chisel, the decorating sins of a multitude of past occupiers were revealed as layer after layer crumbled under the onslaught.

Under the woodchip, there were bright blue and silver stripes; under that, a hideous maroon flock; then an ill-advised brown and orange floral. Who could have lived with any of them, in a room approximately eight foot by eight? Then, blue distemper; then a shiny embossed tan paper; and finally an olive-green oil paint. There were also quite a lot of holes, most of them due to me. It took me all of the rest of Sunday, three broken fingernails and two buckets of hot detergent before it was all off, and when, flushed with exertion and success, I removed the last particle, the dining room looked like a different place. A Dickensian slum.

Up in one corner near the ceiling, the laths showed through, and there was a hole the size of my fist where the central light fitting had once been. Halfway down one side, a rough strip of wood showed where the old mantelshelf had been cut back flush with the plaster. The remaining three walls were liberally pock-marked with depressions of varying depths. Himself, biting back the tears bravely, surveyed the wreck of what, at breakfast, had been quite an attractive little room. 'What've you done?' he whimpered, leaning against the leprous wall in shock. A trickle of powdered plaster showered on to his shoulder, like ancient dandruff. 'I was going to paint *over* that paper, it was the only thing holding the place together.' I looked at him pityingly. How awful, to have gone through life never knowing the heady excitement of wanton destruction. 'You want to try it sometime,' I said, 'it'd work wonders for your tension. Besides,' I added cheeringly, 'it only needs a spot of filling. It shouldn't take you long.'

It took him three weeks of unremitting hard labour before we had a surface in any kind of condition to take paint; and even then we had to use the kind that has gritty bits mixed in, so that it camouflaged the worst bumps. But it does have a certain rural, cottagey sort of charm, as long as you don't brush against it and flay yourself. Or so I tell myself; my mother just thinks it looks lumpy. But then she isn't as shortsighted as I am. One thing I did learn from the episode, though, was that I would *not*, in any circumstances, yield to the same temptation in the hall, on the landing and up the stairs. Not if I wanted to stay friends with Himself, that is. He was a pretty broken man for a while after the trauma of seeing his beloved going berserk, and then having to deal with the aftermath, and I didn't want to push him too far. There was too much other decorating still to do. Besides, tentative proddings of the hall walls had resulted in nasty hollow sounds which meant that there were probably enormous holes lying hidden; it wasn't worth the risk. Goodness knows what we might find. Let sleeping dogs lie, I thought. We still had the bedroom, attic, kitchen and bathroom to tackle. And the attic in particular promised to be a really cathartic experience – the paper was already festooned in fascinating curls where the damp had got in. The chimney wall looked like an antique map – 'Here be dragons.' Something Would Have To Be Done if the room were ever to be habitable.

So I asked around for a roofer; and Mr O'Toole arrived, climbed on to the roof, clomped about dislodging slates, and descended shaking his head pessimistically. 'A death-trap, that chimney thur,' he announced. I pointed out that the roof was rarely crammed with passers-by, and that, quite frankly, anyone using it as a thoroughfare had no one to blame but himself if he tangled with our smoke stack. 'It's leanin',' he explained, 'an' the pointin's gone, forebye. It'll hold for a wee while maybe, and then one day, when the street's full o' weans playin' . . .' He paused, to let me imagine the ghastly scene. 'Sue you they could, for negligence and pain,' he surmised, squinting up at the offending chimney and stepping aside just in case. 'You need the whole thing takin' down and rebuildin', new tiles, new flashin' an' new gutters. There's not a flitter holding the thing together, sure there's not.' 'Are you *sure* it needs all that?' I pleaded. The sellers had assured us that the roof was comparatively new. 'Would I tell you a lie?' he demanded. 'How much?' I asked, getting to the heart of the matter. He removed his duncher, scratched his thick crop of red curls as an aid to cogitation, replaced the duncher and spoke. 'Four hundred pounds,' he said. 'FOUR HUNDRED POUNDS?' I screeched, sending next-door's dog into a frenzy of yapping and causing doors to open all down the street. 'You must be kidding – I can't afford that much, I'll have to get a second opinion . . .' 'Right you be,' said Mr O'Toole, climbing into his lorry. 'But don't be leavin' it too long now; it'd only take a bit of a wind – and me an' the boys could have it done for you by next Tuesday, cash in the hand, no questions asked.' And, with a final doom-laden upward glance, he drove off, leaving me in a welter of indecision. Four hundred pounds! It might as well have been four thousand. But if the chimney fell . . . we might be left with a lawsuit, not to mention a nasty mess in the front garden. I never was very good at the sight of other people's blood.

Himself and I chewed the problem over for the next couple of days, and shook in our shoes and our beds whenever the air was in sensible motion, waiting for the crash and the shriek. Should we approach our friendly local bank manager yet again? It had been cap in hand last time; this time it would have to be sack-cloth and ashes at the very least, possibly with boot-licking and obeisance thrown in. The building society? That would raise the mortgage into the realms of the National Debt. Neither of us had any rich, doting uncles approaching their expiry date. We didn't think we should really count on winning any of the multitude of junk-mail prize draws that tumbled daily through the letter box and which I enthusiastically entered, being a believer in blind fate and a sucker into the bargain. 'There's nothing else for it,' I told Himself. 'It'll have to be the Albert Clock.' The ultimate sacrifice loomed; nothing for it but to exploit the fair white body, as a last desperate resort. The Albert Clock is where the local ladies of easy virtue forgather.

Himself looked shocked. 'Good grief,' he said, 'that'd take far too long – even at fifty p a time you'd be rocking round the clock well into your dotage. We need money *now*.' I was a bit narked at his response; I'd been thinking of a going rate of at least seventy-five pence, or even eighty – after all, the thighs weren't too saggy in a poor light, and the competition was hardly calculated to give Raquel Welch any sleepless nights. Still, he had a point; and I've always thought it must be such a chilly profession, what with all those damp walls you have to stand up against with your skirt hoisted round your waist. 'Think of your arthritis,' said Himself, so we decided against the wages of sin and agreed to risk Mr O'Toole's fearful prophecy and get a second opinion, like an invalid hoping against hope to find someone who will tell him he hasn't got the dreaded lurgy after all.

We found Mr O'Meara. He came, he saw, he pronounced his verdict, and may his memory be hallowed for ever in the annals of sainted roofers. 'Nathin' up there that a wee cowl on the chimney pot won't fix,' he beamed, having tripped all over the roof like a booted fairy. 'Sure yer tiles are as salid as a rack and yer flashin's the same. Two cowls and a perra ventilators in yer roof-space an' yer flyin'.' In disbelief, I relayed Mr O'Toole's prophecy. 'Rabbitch,' he said succinctly, 'yon's a cowboy, he'd rab yer blind so he would. I'll come the marrer and fix it. It's wee buns – four hours and fifty quid'll see it done.' I was so delighted and relieved that before he started work the next day I laced his mug with such a massive slug of whisky that I spent all morning worrying in case he fell off the roof. It could be dangerous, being drunk-in-charge-of-a-ladder.

After that, we had no excuse for putting off the refurbishing, and our expertise grew by leaps and bounds. There was the time we papered the bathroom and found when we'd finished that every alternate strip was hung upside-down; the time we bought a carpet of guaranteed size from a gipsy at the door and unrolled it in the bedroom to find it was three feet short; the time all the carpets had to be lifted for the Rentokil men and I found an amethyst earring, and we relaid the staircarpet from the wrong end and ended up with two bare treads at the bottom rather than the top. There was the occasion when, driven by a strange and foolish desire to have everything clean, I impulsively dismantled the venetian blinds and flung them into a bath full of soapy water. That little exercise lost us a whole weekend; it was like trying to reassemble an exploded octopus. There was the night when, bounding in unbridled lust from one bed to the other, I put one foot through the floorboards and ended up between the joists instead of between the sheets. And the day the fireplace fell down. Himself plastered it all fairly smooth and put up a new mantelshelf, and the next time we had a party a guest leaned elegantly against it and brought the whole thing crashing into the grate – ornaments, drinks, unpaid bills and all. It was the highlight of the evening and livened things up no end.

Not that we didn't thoroughly enjoy our endeavours, even if they weren't always overwhelmingly successful. I was absolutely thrilled to find that Himself not only *let* me paint important bits all by myself, he positively encouraged me to tackle them. Neither did he interfere, or criticise my technique – he kept well out of the way, in fact. It was probably because I was still in a state of besottedness, blind to all faults, that I didn't at first see the sneaky method in his madness; what I painted, he didn't have to. At the time I was simply excited at getting the chance; in the past I'd never graduated from the window frames, which were dull and fiddly but where I couldn't do a great deal of harm.

The kitchen ceiling was my first big solo endeavour, and it was while I was standing on the table, with a crick in my neck and a pint of buttercup gloss dripping from my right elbow, that the first doubts crept in. Was it supposed to hurt as much as this? Were you supposed to get a sleeveful of paint, and if so did one allow for it when calculating quantities? Would Himself still love me, with punky yellow-striped hair? Would I ever get my head upright again, or was I fated to spend the rest of my life surveying the heavens, like those Indian fakirs who fix their eyes on the sun until they go blind? The ceiling, which had started off quite small, seemed to be increasing in acreage by the minute. My arms ached unbearably, the paint went on either too thick or too thin, I kept seeing bits I'd missed and having to go back to fill them in, which meant shoving the table to and fro or clambering on to the draining board. After I'd trodden unexpectedly into the sink twice and hit my funnybone on a cupboard handle once, the thrill of it all was fading fast and my admiration for Michelangelo knew no bounds. Although, come to think of it, he hadn't had a sink to contend with and at least he'd been able to lie down on the job.

Unwisely, I spun round to reach an awkward corner, with my head still nestling cosily between my shoulder-blades. The room suddenly tilted alarmingly, and 'Help!' I bleated – vertigo threatened urgently and it was quite a nasty drop from table to floor. Himself came in from the hall, where he was contentedly chipping paint off the banisters. 'What's up?' he asked, steadying me as I swayed dizzily and getting an earful of gloss for his pains. 'I feel all swimmy,' I panted, 'and my right arm's all soggy. I think I've discovered a new disease – Painter's Armpit.' 'What *you* need,' Himself advised, helping me down off the table and propping me against a wall, 'is half a tennis ball.' 'Oh ah?' I replied uncomprehendingly. I was beyond rational thought. 'Yes,' he explained, disappearing into the cupboard under the stairs to rummage for the moth-eaten ball which was a relic of Lucy Kitten's short stay. 'What you do,' his muffled voice emerged as he dredged through the dross in the cupboard, 'is cut the ball in half and stick the paintbrush handle oh bloody hell' – here he cracked his head on the stairs – '*through* it, so it's in a sort of cup and the paint goes in there, and it can't run down your arm. Here you are!' He backed out triumphant and dusty, with the ball.

'I'll cut it in half for you and stick the handle through,' he offered kindly, 'you'll find the job much easier after that.' I gazed at the ceiling, with its uneven stripes of blotchy colour. I eyed the floor, a disaster area with its collage of torn newspaper and spilt paint superimposed on the usual grime. I looked down at my ruined sweater and jeans, and blew a lank buttercup lock out of my eye. Finally I surveyed Himself, standing there all eager to do his bit by cutting a tennis ball in half for me. And I told him that in my opinion, there was only one place that I'd like him to stick the paintbrush handle before he took his turn at the blasted ceiling. At least the paint wouldn't trickle down his arm. With or without half a tennis ball.

This uncharitable response to my beloved's offer of help was, I tried to reassure him later, only because I was under stress. Perhaps we were trying to do too much at once, which admittedly was mostly my fault because of my penchant for stripping. Once laid bare, a room can't be left naked for long; it's very depressing, and visitors are apt to look what I can only describe as askance. So I had to give it up. It was almost like trying to give up smoking – no use cutting down and limiting yourself to one piece of wallpaper a day. It was all or nothing. It was a wrench, and took tons of willpower, but eventually I beat the addiction, although for ages, when we went to other people's houses, my eye was drawn irresistibly to any little loose bit on the wall, and my fingers would creep towards it of their own volition. The first six weeks were the worst, but since then I have gone without completely; I know that it would only take one slip and there I'd be, back on four walls a day, hooked.

We didn't spend *all* our time on the delights of domestic decoration, of course. Outside the home, life went on as usual – work, shopping, social life when we weren't too tired or too covered in paint. I had decided that temping, although interesting, was too precarious an occupation for one half of a partnership that needed money as much as we did; one week I was in work and the next I'd be stranded at home, gnawing my nails and dreading the non-arrival of a pay cheque the following week. A permanent post was the only answer, and as well as botching the decorating I was sending out letters of application in all directions, and rigging my curriculum vitae so that I looked a bit more respectable. Prospective employers faced with a record of over twenty jobs in as many years are likely to regard the applicant in the same way that our visitors regarded our walls. Definitely askance. Pointing out that I'd never been sacked, always left of my own accord and usually because of a family move cut very little ice. Obviously I was marked with the stigma of the undependable roamer, the scorner of pension rights; and as such, I was not the most desirable of employees.

Worst of all, of course, I was The Wrong Age. I was The Wrong Side of Forty, Over the Hill. In other words, I had the necessary skills and experience and expected a corresponding salary. So it wasn't easy, what with one thing and another; I was now spending my lunchtimes not rushing to view houses but rushing to interviews if I was lucky enough to be granted one. Nothing came of any of them, except a couple of offers of junior's work at junior's salaries; and I was on the point of taking one of those when a turn-up for the book occurred. I was asked to return permanently to one of the places where I had previously temped for a while; I'd enjoyed it there, the 'crack' had been good and interesting. Before the month was out, I was once more gainfully employed and acquiring a skill I'd never attempted before, which was immensely satisfying after being told in interviews that 'at my age' I couldn't be expected to learn new techniques. I became an offset litho printing press operator, turning out posters, hand-outs, student newspapers, tickets; you name it I printed it. I learnt how to make plates, how to photograph copy, how to lift enormous wodges of heavy paper on to the machine all day, how to stand for six hours at a stretch until my veins screamed for relief, how to cover myself from head to foot in printing ink, how to trap my fingers between the rollers. Most of all, I learned how to be more physically exhausted by the end of the day than I would have believed possible. Which led, indirectly, to a major change in our lives. If I'd had my wits about me, on that one particular evening . . .

Away with the Fairies

Himself arrived home one Friday evening and enquired, with the air of one who already fears the answer, whether his dress-shirt was clean. From the depths of the sofa, where I was lying work-worn, week-weary and press-stressed, I replied yes, surprise surprise, yah boo sucks to you, is it another Masonic do? It was approaching winter, when Himself's life is one long social whirl of Masonic dinners, fancy-dress parties, all-boys-together outings, while the wives and hangers-on are lumbered with the food-providing, the regalia-cleaning and the hangover-curing. 'Goodness, no,' said Himself, and reminded me that tonight was the big annual do at the yacht club – 'I told you *weeks* ago,' he said reproachfully. My sluggish brain, pounded to the consistency of semolina by the noise of my machine, threw up a vague memory of Himself explaining that the Fairy Dinner Dance was *not*, as I had envisaged, a gathering of gnarled yachtsmen clad in tutus, limp-wristed and wand-waving, but a social nosh-up for those mad enough to spend their time, money and energy getting soaked to the skin in Fairy-class yachts. And it was *tonight* . . .

My eyelids, formerly shut with the finality of the Lubyanka gates, flew open and I left the sofa in a vertical take-off, propelled by shock waves. I made a one-point landing, catching my shin on the coffee table, and hobbled upstairs in total panic, clutching my bleeding leg. Himself shouted that the taxi would arrive at 8.30. I had two hours to wreak a miracle, render myself glamorous, lively, amusing, sparkling . . .

My reflection in the bathroom mirror caused despair to rise like the neap tide; the morning's mascara had settled into the plentiful lines around my eyes. I looked like a hung-over panda. My skin had all the glow of yesterday's porridge. My nails were rimmed with printers' ink like a Victorian mourning card. I considered developing a sudden blinding migraine, or leprosy, or yaws – but the tickets were already bought at bankrupting expense and my innate streak of meanness surfaced. I would have to go, even if I resembled a survivor from a Siberian labour camp.

I turned on the water and underwent a brisk therapeutic shower, during which the second shock wave hit my battle-fatigued brain – where was my Sole Evening Dress? The SED, bought at rock-bottom price from the reject basket of the local dress emporium, had last been worn at a previous year's jollification; I could vaguely remember peeling it off in a drunken daze, treading in the hem in the process and then, clad in high heels, tights and alcoholic virtue, putting it away – *where*? I reeled out of the shower and, dripping wet, ransacked the house, calling on heaven, Himself, *anyone*, for help. None was forthcoming. Eventually I unearthed the SED at the bottom of the spare-room wardrobe, crumpled into a ball, the hem down, an unidentifiable but sinister stain on the skirt. What was I to do? There was no chance to visit my usual couturiers – Oxfam, War on Want, where were you when I needed you?

Luckily the dress was extremely rude – hence only tights and high heels – in fact the whole thing was so skimpy that a quick rinse in the bath followed by half an hour in the tumble dryer would have it as good as new. Well, as good as second-hand. Himself, calmly changing in the bedroom, looked at his watch and wisely said nothing. Yet. An hour to go before blast-off – my dress was still in the dryer, and my hair had meantime dried into an unkempt birds' nest. There was no time to put in rollers; I looked as if I'd stuck my finger in the light socket. Never mind – the important thing was to find my decent evening shoes, the ones that weren't down at heel. They were in the water-tank cupboard, I could see them in my mind's eye, in *one* of the boxes stacked up there. But which one? I spent a much-needed ten minutes flinging everything out on to the attic floor before I found them. In the bottom box, naturally, and filthy. I raced downstairs for the suede brush and broke a nail on the shoe-polish box in my frantic haste. I cursed the box. More haste less speed, said Himself, sitting smugly in the living room with a sherry in his hand. I cursed Himself.

Tights! Tights! I had to have tights! There must be an unladdered pair somewhere, I thought. I distinctly remember buying a pair not so long ago . . . I hurled the contents of my underwear drawer out over my shoulder. Red tights, blue tights, green, black, yellow and purple tights – where the bloody hell were my *beige* tights? Hysteria was imminent, and the house was beginning to look as if a cyclone had hit it. I tore the drawer from its foundations and discovered an unopened packet of beige tights crammed down the back.

Twenty minutes until the taxi arrived. Himself was on his second sherry and I was on my first tranquilliser. I dragged on the tights, crammed my feet into the shoes, squeezed myself into the dress; the zip took a spiteful nip out of my back. I can't have put on all *that* much weight

in the past year, I thought frantically, I'd forgotten this dress was *that* indecent. Never mind, I'll just have to hold my breath all night. For once I was grateful that I wasn't built like Dolly Parton.

Now there was only my face to deal with. A daunting prospect. I hoped the lights at the Yacht Club were tactfully dim and that the other guests' eyesight would be in the same condition by the time we arrived. I slapped on foundation, lashed on the blusher, and ladled on the eyeshadow; perhaps we could find a nice dark corner. I

133

wished the Fairy Dinner Dance were a masked ball. With no unmasking at midnight. My hair was past all hope. I bunged on gel to plaster it back and put on the biggest earrings I could find, to distract the eye of the beholder. Ready. I looked in the bedroom mirror. What had happened to the beautiful sophisticate intended for the evening? What had happened to the dewy youthfulness of bygone years? It was bygone, that's what.

I tottered downstairs as the taxi sounded its horn, and asked rather stupidly how I looked. Himself, with his eyes carefully averted, said fine, come on for goodness' sake, the taxi meter is ticking over like a demented metronome running up a bill you wouldn't believe. I reflected that Himself's mean streak was even wider than mine. I flung on my daytime overcoat – there was no time to find my evening wrap – and got into the taxi. And then remembered that my hem was still down.

I rushed back into the house and grabbed the first cotton-reel in the box, impaling my finger smartly on the attached needle, and returned to the waiting taxi, shattered. I was now bleeding from (a) my shin, (b) my finger and (c) the zip nip. Thank heavens my dress was red; I'd probably be the first ever person to drop dead from loss of blood during a Fairy Dinner Dance in the entire history of the Yacht Club. I spent the journey regaining my breath and sewing up the hem in the dark. I discovered later that the cotton was blue, but by then there was no point in worrying about it. We arrived at the club gates and paid the astronomical taxi fare, and I realised I was bereft of handbag, comb, lipstick, cash, hanky, tranquillisers – they were all at home, lying handily on the hall table. A vision of my first gin floated tantalisingly into my mind's eye, and the vision of a second one even more so.

We walked up the drive, the gravel penetrating the thin soles of my shoes painfully with every step. Through the club window I could see blessedly dim lights; and then discerned the figures within. A bored barman yawning, solitary optimist shoving coins into the games machine, resident alcoholic in his usual corner. No one else. Where were the laughing crowds, the friends, the gaiety, balloons, music, streamers, here-we-go and there-we-go? Where the champagne-filled galoshes, the brandy-filled sou'westers? Where, in short, was the Fairy Dinner Dance? Himself perused the tickets and read out the date. The 29th. Today was the 22nd. The bloody Fairy Dinner Dance wasn't until next week . . .

Oh dear, said Himself nonchalantly, I must have misread the date when I first looked at the tickets. Never mind, he went on, we can always come back next week. It should give you more time to get ready, and perhaps you'll be able to unearth a dress more suited to your years. As we're here, he added, we might as well have a drink – would you like a gin?

With terrible control I said yes – *several*, preferably doubles. I couldn't trust myself to say anything else. Yet. I followed Himself up the steps to the club door in a grim and pregnant silence. On the third step, I tripped and caught my heel in my dress hem.

As it turned out, it took several gins before I was capable of coherent thought, let alone speech. The evening lay in shreds around us. There was no reason to stay on at the club once I had recovered; where was the sense in paying for our drinks when we had a perfectly good bottle at home just crying out for a bit of love and attention? We trailed home again in our – my – bedraggled finery and settled down by the fire for an evening of good old-fashioned home entertainment. And I must admit it turned out to be very much more fun than any dance could have been. By the time the level in the gin bottle had sunk past the label, we had comprehensively exhausted the subjects that always arise on these occasions – the future of mankind in a technological age, the likelihood of personal survival after death, the houseplants, and whether or not we'd ever be able to afford new carpets – and got on to our particular favourite, which is how delightful each other is. This fascinating topic held us spellbound until the gin seemed somehow to have mysteriously evaporated, which caused a brief hiatus in the conversation while Himself hunted down our carefully hidden bottle of ouzo. By this time I couldn't have cared less if I never got to a Fairy Dinner Dance again; this was much cosier, and I could take my shoes off, too.

In fact, I needn't stop at the shoes – I could unzip and relax, an excellent idea which was greeted by cheers all round. It was but the work of several moments – my foot kept getting stuck in the coal scuttle – to remove the tights, too. Himself became aware that he too felt overdressed in his reefer jacket, and soon we were having a very pleasant evening indeed. The time flew by, and I betted Himself that we were having a far more enjoyable time than anyone else we knew. 'You could be right,' he said, after long consideration. 'I bet none of them is sitting on the hearth rug in front of the fire, drinking ouzo. And certainly not wearing earrings.' I disputed this. '*Most* of our women friends wear earrings,' I pointed out. '*Just?*' he said, and we somehow lost the thread of our conversation all together as events took an even more absorbing turn. The Fairy Fiasco faded, unnoticed and unmourned, into the past.

* * *

It was 3 am before we finally climbed the stairs, only slightly unsteadily, and got into bed. We cuddled up in silence, broken only by little mmms of affection as we got settled into the most comfortable position for sleep. 'That was a *lovely* night after all,' I murmured into Himself's back, as I hugged him round the waist. 'We must do it again sometime.' 'Good idea,' he agreed, 'it's a great place for a party. Do you come here often?' 'Oh, nearly always, thank you,' I assured him. 'Shall we make a date for next Friday then?' he asked sleepily. 'I'll see if I'm free,' I said. 'And if I haven't got a previous engagement, it's a definite date.' He turned over and put his arms round me. 'Perhaps we *should* make a definite date,' he said, and kissed me. Then he climbed out of bed and left the room. I thought he was just going to the loo, and snuggled down, putting my legs over into the warm place where he had been. Then I heard him going right on down the stairs and into the sitting room – had he left his tobacco pouch downstairs and if so, why did he want it now? I heard him coming back up, and turned on the bedside light to see if the pouch was on the side table; he lost it regularly and it was usually lying out in plain view in the most obvious place. Sure enough, there it was, and as he came back into the bedroom I opened my mouth to ask him why he hadn't looked there in the first place.

At the sight of him, however, my mouth remained open but nothing came out. There he stood, clad in his watch, clutching a chrysanthemum in his hand. I sat up in bed in some alarm. Had the ouzo had some sort of delayed-action effect on his wits? What was he going to do with the chrysanthemum? He smiled at me; he certainly didn't look loopy, but you never knew. Then he came over to the bed and, very naturally and unselfconsciously and with only the tiniest of wobbles, went down on one knee.

137

He held the flower out towards me. 'Will you marry me?' he asked.

I looked at him kneeling there, offering me the chrysanthemum and marriage, and all sorts of thoughts raced through my mind, which had suddenly become stone-cold sober. Marriage had never been one of our subjects of discussion; it had never seemed important. We were perfectly happy as we were. Would it change things, spoil them in some way as I'd seen it do with other couples who had lived together in perfect harmony, only to drift apart once the knot was tied? Was I prepared to commit myself again, to lose my precious independence, to tie myself down? Was Himself, after so many years of bachelorhood, really fitted to become a husband? Would it change him, would he suddenly start expecting ironed shirts and clean socks and a cooked breakfast, and a wife who was always there and didn't just take off for a while when she felt like it? Would it change me into someone who expected a husband to be someone who didn't go out with the boys any more, who resented being left alone while he went off to pursue his sporting interests? All this flashed through my brain in less than five seconds – and I knew without any doubt that marriage wouldn't make any difference at all, except to make us belong to each other even more. So – 'Oh, yes, please,' I said, and fell out of bed into his arms.

When I woke up in the morning, very late, I wondered if it had really happened – had I really received and accepted a proposal of marriage at 3 am that morning? I nudged Himself and he opened the eye that wasn't buried in the pillow. 'Did you really ask me to marry you?' I asked. 'I did,' he grunted – he's never at his best in the mornings, but who is? 'And did I say yes?' I went on, just to make sure. 'You did,' he said. 'And do you still want to?' I persisted – after all, the sight of me in the sober light of day might well be enough to make any man in his right mind renege. 'I do,' he said, and closed the eye again. 'Not,' he muttered into the pillow, 'that I mightn't change my mind unless you can rustle up a life-saving cup of nice hot tea within the next five minutes.'

I smote him with my pillow, just to teach him to mind his manners, jumped out of bed before he could retaliate and leapt downstairs to put the kettle on. The sun was shining and it was a beautiful day.

Our friends' reactions to our momentous news were mixed, and not always expected. His bachelor friends greeted it as a sad downfall for one of their number, a breaching of the defences, almost an occasion for commiseration. 'Thought it was too good to last,' said one gloomily. 'Another good lad gone, caught, trapped before his time.' Frankly, I thought Himself had had a jolly good run for his money – he'd managed to evade the bonds of matrimony for a good half-century, which was fair going even by Ulster standards. Others sympathised with me, which was nice. 'It won't be easy,' warned one well-meaning lady. 'After all, he's been used to having his own way for so long. He'll be hard to change, mark my words.' Changing him was the last thing I had in mind, but she seemed to see marriage as something along the lines of dog-obedience classes. 'Set in his ways,' said another, darkly, 'going to the club and so on, you'll have a job on your hands.' Obviously she saw it as a case for The Love of a Good Woman, which would turn a carefree bachelor into a careworn spouse. 'What do you want to get *married* for?' asked a not-particularly-happily-married workmate of mine. 'You must be mad, tying yourself down – now if *I* had *my* time over again . . .'

But the prophets of doom were, happily, in the minority. All our closest friends were gratifyingly delighted. As one of them said – the lovely large cuddly man who had first made me feel so at home in Belfast – 'It's the best news I've heard in years – the best thing in the world for yer man, and for you too. You're made for each other, so you are.' 'Terrific!' said the others. 'When's it going to be?' which was a detail we hadn't thought about – we were still too busy just getting used to the idea. 'As soon as possible,' I decided, and from then on we were caught up in a whirl of activity for the next few weeks. It's surprising how much there is to arrange, even for the small quiet affair which we planned.

For one thing, there was the reception to book. Not that that posed any problem; there was only one venue where we could possibly have it. After all, it was their fault in the first place. It had to be the Yacht Club. They were entirely to blame for the Workman Wedding.

I Do! I Do!

Apart from the matter of the reception, which presented no problem, there turned out to be all sorts of other things to arrange, about most of which we knew absolutely nothing. Himself, of course, had never before entered the Tender Trap, and my previous experience had been long ago and far away when I was very young, and had my head so full of moonlight and roses that the actual preliminaries to tying the knot, as far as I was concerned, were limited to my dress, my flowers and how soon we could get on honeymoon. Doubtless my parents had dealt with all the necessary legal requirements then but this time it was up to us. Or rather me, to be honest; Himself works out of town and in any case I preferred to do it myself. Having got this far, it would never do to have him chickening out at the last minute. I wanted to be quite sure of making an honest man of him.

So I unearthed all the relevant papers to prove we were both free, allegedly in our right minds and well over the age of consent, and made the arrangements with the register office. Then we had to have the notice of forthcoming marriage inserted in the newspaper for the requisite number of times, which led to my getting to know a neighbour whom previously I had only seen to wave to from time to time as I left for work. The evening after the notice first appeared, she shot out of her front door as I passed by on my way home and waylaid me. She was a

typical Belfast matriarch, a tiny tough old lady of strong
religious convictions who spent her days in a constant
battle against grime, which had her out sweeping the
pavement and polishing her front path and shaking rugs

punitively against the back-alley walls. This evening, as
usual, she had her curlers in, her teeth out and her pinny
on and she was hell-bent on buttonholing me. 'I see youse
is gettin' married,' she cried, flashing her gums at me in
congratulation and automatically dusting the gatepost as
she spoke. 'Seen it in the paper, I did. I said to my man I
said, themuns at number 82 is gettin' wed, isn't that great!'
I was a trifle apprehensive. After all, we'd been living
alongside her in what she doubtless considered sin for

143

several months. Was I about to get a lecture on morality? I needn't have worried. 'Pleased as Punch we are,' she continued, 'to see youse was both Protestants forbye, because' – here she lowered her voice and glanced up and down the street – 'this here side of the street's always been Protestant, so it has. I've nothin' against themuns across the way – but this is *our* side, always was, from when I was just a wee wain . . .' 'How did you know?' I asked. There had been no mention of religious affiliation in the notice of marriage. 'Didn't it say you was divorced?' she explained. 'Sure when I seen that, I said to my man, yer woman's a good Protestant craytur . . .' It was nice to know I'd done at least something to gain the neighbours' approval.

Even if they weren't of the same consuming importance as the first time around, my dress and flowers did have to be thought of. I decided to pay Himself the compliment of actually buying a new outfit for the occasion; charity-shop dressing is all very well for everyday, but I felt I was justified in lashing out on something first-hand in the circumstances. (Mind you, I had a precautionary zoom round my old haunts first, just in case someone had left in a once-worn Jaeger or even a misfit Emmanuel, but no one had.) No, I wouldn't stint myself – if I saw the perfect outfit then blow the expense this once. And within three days I saw it, in the window of one of those small, exclusive, terrifying boutiques where they put one dress and a single item of super upmarket costume jewellery in the window, and no price tags because if they did you'd be too stunned to go in.

Oh, it was gorgeous – fine black silk with a dropped waistline and swirling cross-cut skirt, the bloused bodice covered in printed red poppies, the whole thing flowing and elegant and very 1930s . . . It was exactly what I would have dreamed about if I'd had the right kind of imagination. I floated into the boutique on waves of total infatuation and managed to gain the attention of one of the sales staff; she was terribly cut-glass, about six foot three tall with immaculate paintwork and prepubertal hips, and she probably thought I'd come in to do the vacuuming. There followed a very brief exchange between us and in a trice I was back on the pavement and far from floating. The price of the dream-creation was roughly equivalent to six months' mortgage repayments. Sunk in gloom, I turned away to retrace my steps to the Help the Aged shop; perhaps they might have had a new consignment since I last looked.

But in the end I didn't have to be a Second-hand Rose after all. Halfway to H the A, my eye was caught by a huge notice proclaiming 'Positively all Stock MUST GO!' emblazoned across a shop front, which is how I came to be wed in a very classic, very serviceable and quite flattering beige two-piece. I missed the poppies, though.

Poppies weren't in season at the florists', either; at that time of year it was roses or nothing. I had decided to give my valuable custom – one little bouquet and two buttonholes – to a newly opened shop run by a young couple; I felt they might well take a more personal interest, having just started up. The husband was very attentive as I outlined what I wanted – a small posy, nothing ostentatious, just something pretty yet discreet. 'I understand,' he nodded sympathetically, making notes in his book. 'Naturally you wouldn't want anything too young and girlish. Don't worry, madam, I'll make sure the bouquet is suitable to a mature bride like yourself – someone of more advanced years, as you might say.' And, smiling understandingly, he ushered his doddering customer from the premises.

To give credit where it's due, he turned in a very good job. However, my misgivings about his future prospects in the field of bridal floristry were fulfilled when, six months later, he went out of business. Someone should have told him that florists need to learn how to flatter. Their stock isn't the only thing that needs to be flowery.

The next matter to be decided was that of witnesses. It was easy for Himself, because he'd lived there such a long time; he simply coerced an old school chum into doing the deed. But I had no such friend to stand up for me. I thought about it for a while and then asked Barbara. Barbara worked with me and we got on like a house on fire, despite her being about half my age. She was a lovely, lively, funny girl with a beautiful mane of dark, thick hair which she enthusiastically tinted vibrant plum, and a perfect complexion in defiance of a diet which appeared to consist of very little more than a surfeit of cream-filled chocolate eggs. She was great company and we spent many a happy ten minutes at the office window, surveying the passing male talent and awarding marks out of ten for such attributes as length of leg and neatness of bum. To my delight, she was thrilled to bits to be a sort of bridesmaid, and was a great help. Because of the ravages of the printing press, my nails were in a shocking state – if they grew longer than a millimetre they got broken, and they were always black. There was no chance of their being presentable on The Day, and Barbara suggested false ones. On Day Minus Two she came round to help me put them on, and we had a lovely evening; Himself was at his stag party, and between the nail glue and a litre of best plonk we had a grand time. 'Easy to fix – beautiful new fingernails in half an hour' claimed the legend on the box. Easy-peasy, we thought, and got stuck in at seven o'clock.

By nine, we were still struggling; the blasted nails adhered to everything but where they were supposed to go. We filed and glued and cursed and held our breaths and had another glass of wine; and then we glued again and spent five minutes extricating an errant false nail from the sheepskin hearthrug and had another drink to give us strength. At long last, by eleven o'clock I had ten beautiful new nails, as promised. Some of them a bit skew-wiff, admittedly, but they were all cemented firmly into place. I felt like Fu Manchu. Gratefully, I poured the last of the wine into Barbara's glass. 'I'd never have managed without you,' I said. 'Well, mind how you go tomorrow,' she advised, draining the wine and unsticking her fingers from the glass. 'Don't be struggling too much if there's any horseplay – I couldn't face having to fix another set.'

'What d'you mean?' I quavered, 'they wouldn't really, would they? Not to a bride of advanced years? Oh Barbara, promise me – if anything happens, help me!' 'Right you be,' said my bridesmaid, getting up and preparing for home, 'but tell me this and tell me no more – do you think they'll let you off scot-free? But here dear, I don't think they'll go too far, not with you not being used to that kind of thing.' And with that slight comfort, she left me to my imaginings.

You have to understand that in Ulster, brides-to-be have a tough time of it. The custom still prevails, as no doubt it does elsewhere too, of subjecting the poor girl to the sort of humiliating experience I'd thought was undergone only by apprentices to the more robust trades. I'd been in Belfast a week when I first came across it in practice. There in the middle of town, in Albert Square itself, was a girl stripped to her petticoat, with a makeshift net head-dress on and covered from head to foot in flour and lipstick. She was tied into a supermarket trolley, and across her chest was a sign bearing an extremely indelicate message. The perpetrators of this painful spectacle, her co-workers in the supermarket, stood a short way off, shrieking with laughter and passing highly censorable comments on the forthcoming honeymoon. I was appalled – the poor girl! she must be mortified – until I saw that far from being upset, she was screaming with laughter too, throwing handsful of flour at passers-by and generally giving the impression of loving every minute of her ordeal. If that ever happened to me, I thought, I'd *die* of embarrassment . . . and now Barbara thinks there might be a possibility of it. Oh God, I don't think I'll go to work tomorrow, I'll spend the day in the cupboard under the stairs . . .

I couldn't, of course. But it was a very apprehensive woman who went off to work that day, like a lamb to the slaughter. All morning, nothing happened. Lunchtime passed uneventfully. Half the afternoon went by peacefully. I stopped twitching and began to relax. Tea time arrived, and with it more girls than usual congregated in the office. I skulked in the print room – they were up to something, oh heavens . . . They called me, in bright, nonchalant, untrustworthy tones. I braced myself. *Please*, I prayed silently, don't let them strip me to my undies – I was saving the good ones for our honeymoon and my bra wasn't a pretty sight. I took a deep breath and entered the office – and suddenly it was all confetti and hugs and kisses and presents and wine, and nothing to be nervous about at all. My bra wasn't to be exposed to public ridicule after all. Through the showers of confetti I caught Barbara's eye. 'Didn't I tell you they wouldn't let you off scot-free?' she giggled, and handed me a glass of champagne.

We were still celebrating when the junior came back from answering the buzzer and said there was a gentleman to see me. Himself, I thought, how lovely, he's got off work early and come to pick me up. I dashed out to bring him in, but it wasn't Himself – it was a stranger. 'Someone to see you downstairs,' he announced, 'he can't manage the stairs, would you come down to him please?' Mystified, I excused myself from the girls and the stranger took my hand firmly and led me downstairs and outside to the street. And there was Himself – and no wonder he couldn't manage the stairs. He was clad in a long Victorian nightgown, he was covered with talcum powder and lipstick, he was roped into a wheelchair hung with banners proclaiming 'I'm only doing it for the Tax Rebate!' and 'No one in the typing pool would have me!', to quote two of the polite ones. A pair of red shiny Christmas tree baubles were pinned fetchingly just the appropriate distance below the waist of the nightgown. They had brought him all the way into town in the back of an open station wagon, with all lights blazing and the horn blaring, and then pushed him at breakneck speed up and down the streets in the wheelchair. He was crimson from embarrassment and mirth. I collapsed on the steps and laughed until I cried – all I could think of was, thank goodness he put on his good underpants this morning.

In contrast to all that excitement and bubble, The Day itself started off positively sombrely. We exercised enormous amounts of willpower the night before, to make up for all the office jollifications, and spent a virtuously abstemious evening quietly by the fireside. Himself was still recovering from the rigours of his involuntary ride, and I concentrated on varnishing my new talons in between asking Himself every five minutes whether he had the ring in a safe place, and whether he was sure he wanted to go through with it, and how it wasn't too late even now to change his mind, if he didn't mind spending the next few months in a plaster cast. He bore with it all patiently, and took the precaution of putting the jeweller's box on the hall table, ready for the morning. I was very pleased with the ring. To begin with we'd wanted to use one inherited from Himself's aunt, but cutting it to fit would have meant destroying the message engraved inside, so I wear that one on my thumb. But I didn't want a modern new one. The jeweller produced oodles of old ones for me to look at – where had they all come from, where were all the people to whom they had once been so significant? – and I found the very one. It was broad and thick, and when I looked inside I could see it was made from three old rings welded together; I would love to know its history. I liked the idea of it being triple-strength. With my record, it would need to be.

The sombreness of The Day manifested itself immediately in the unusual silence as we got up. As I've said before, Himself is never exactly in sparkling form in the mornings, but I'm usually horribly bright and gay and am even given to singing, which says a lot for Himself's fortitude and forbearance. Not this morning, though. This was It – W-Day, the final commitment. We drank our tea and had our baths and tried to make light conversation. 'Two hours to go,' I informed Himself, who was sitting on the edge of his bed putting his socks on inside-out. 'Don't *tell* me,' he groaned ungallantly, looking at his watch and biting his pipestem so hard it nearly broke. 'Ought we to have something to eat?' I suggested. 'It's a long time until the reception.' 'Condemned man's last meal,' Himself muttered, so I gave up and went to start dressing. Let him make himself something if he was hungry. I knew for a fact that there was nothing in the fridge except a bowl of dripping and two rashers of desiccated bacon, because of going away. If he wanted eggs, let him go up to the corner shop and buy eggs. I was definitely getting edgy. My nerves were like piano wires.

I concentrated hard on getting dressed and putting on a brave face. My hair wouldn't go right and my new shoes were agonising, but once I'd got the hat on I looked quite presentable. I went downstairs to where Himself was standing in the living room, gazing blankly out of the window and working out the quickest escape route. 'Do I look all right?' I asked, and this time he didn't avert his eyes. 'You look beautiful,' he said, so I knew he wasn't himself and was indeed feeling the tension too. Compliments don't spring lightly to his lips. 'So do you,' I said, and we paced up and down the room like two tigers in a cage. After several lengths of the carpet, Himself looked at me desperately as we passed each other and said hoarsely, 'I'm going to have a whisky. Will you take one?' 'Oh yes please,' I pleaded. 'I'm terrified, it's ridiculous, my hands are shaking.' Himself gave me a mirthless smile. 'My knees are,' he told me. 'I haven't been this nervous since the war.' He brought us the drinks and we toasted each other. I looked at my watch again. 'Almost time,' I said. Himself looked out of the window. 'There's John with the car,' he announced, 'this is it. Here we go, love,' and we gathered ourselves together and went out to get married. We were halfway to the City Hall before we had to turn round and go back for the box on the hall table.